GREAT

AMERICAN

BASEBALL

STORIES

LYONS PRESS CLASSICS

GREAT AMERICAN BASEBALL STORIES

EDITED BY
JEFF SILVERMAN

GUILFORD
CONNECTICUT

An imprint of The Rowman & Littlefield Publishing Group, Inc.
4501 Forbes Blvd., Ste. 200
Lanham, MD 20706
www.rowman.com

Distributed by NATIONAL BOOK NETWORK

British Library Cataloguing in Publication Information available

Library of Congress Cataloging-in-Publication Data available

ISBN 978-1-4930-3901-2 (paperback)
ISBN 978-1-4930-3383-6 (e-book)

♾™ The paper used in this publication meets the minimum requirements
of American National Standard for Information Sciences—Permanence of
Paper for Printed Library Materials, ANSI/NISO Z39.48-1992.

Printed in the United States of America

To the Men of Claw ...

Rarae aves, most of them ...

CONTENTS

INTRODUCTION

What's the essential quality that turns a baseball story into a *classic* baseball story? Let's touch base for a moment with America's other national pastime: the movies.

Every year, the American Film Institute hands out a Life Achievement Award to an honoree whose work—so the AFI's Solons assure us—has stood, or will stand, the test of time. What a nice sound—the test of time—and what an exacting criterion. To satisfy it, the work must certainly have legs—like Cobb and Brock and Ricky Henderson; personality—like Ruth and Stengel; power—like Big Mac and the Big Train; craft—like Koufax and Mathewson; grace—like DiMaggio and Williams; courage—like Robinson and Aaron; durability—like Ripken and Ryan; and character—like Clemente and Gehrig. As commendable, individually, as these qualities certainly are, they need more than themselves alone to pass the test; each needs at least a touch of the other. To be classic, in short, is a tall order.

Each of the twenty-two tales—the fictions and the facts—that make up *Classic Baseball Stories* has stood this test of time. They all satisfy the most readily measured threshold—legs—with ease. The baby in the group—Gerald Beaumont's "The Crab"—was first published in 1921, and if we keep the comparison to the movies in play, that puts it squarely in the silent era. Indeed, the majority of the selections that follow gave voice to a game before the movies realized they had any voice at all. They are tales from a time when Cobb and Speaker were hitting .400, when Johnson and Matty (a contributor here, at least in name; his observations about player superstitions were actually penned by sportswriter John Wheeler) were moving 'em down, and when artists like Chaplin and Keaton and D. W. Griffith were taking cuts and making cuts, inventing, as they went along, the grammar of the movies frame by frame.

It was a good time for invention, those days, and in their own way, writers like Ring Lardner, Damon Runyon, Grantland Rice, Zane Grey (yes, *that* Zane Grey, a helluva college outfielder, by the way), Charles Van Loan, and even P. G. Wodehouse (more associated with a small, dimpled ball than one of horsehide stitched together) were also busy making up the language and syntax of the baseball story as they went along. With their pens and their typewriters, they would teach us a new way of seeing and experiencing America's game; reaching into its heart, they pulled out what would become the ever more sophisticated language of baseball on the page. There's magic in that accomplishment to be sure, and the best way to fall under its spell is to continue reading what they batted out. Granted, some of their words and phrases and idioms feel dated—what doesn't after a century or so of service—but that hardly matters, because what they discovered about the game and its hold over us—fans and players alike—is as fresh and excited as busher's face the first time he puts his Major League polyesters on. Keaton and Chaplin are still funny; so are Lardner and Wodehouse. They're old, sure, but their bones don't creak. What they've set down remains energetic and bright, keenly observed and keenly wrought. All these decades later, the words continue to tingle.

Of course, when you understand human nature and baseball nature—as these writers did—the work doesn't really age, just the paper it's printed on. New generations may find more dazzling or sophisticated ways to say things, as new generations of filmmakers keep upping the ante on their special effects, but is what they're revealing to us about who we are any sharper, clearer, more incisive or passionate? A home run is a home run whenever it's hit.

Let me suggest one more connection that ties the early days of baseball writing to the early days of motion pictures: There's a history, memory and sheer enjoyment that's lost when we fail to preserve and keep contact with the legacy handed down to us.

Twenty years ago, when I was a novice screenwriter, I became friends with an older writer-director named Richard Brooks. In the late 1950s, he created one of the most memorable on-screen fires in his classic—I use that word with no reservations at all—adaptation of *Elmer Gantry*. Since the blazing tabernacle scene climaxing the movie would be shot indoors on a soundstage, every inch of the set had been treated with heavy fire retardant before the cameras rolled. Starting a fire 20,000 leagues under the sea would have been a snap by comparison.

Naturally, Brooks couldn't get the flames to go, so he asked the fire marshal on set what to do. The answer stunned the filmmaker. The fire marshal told him to raid the studio vault, pull out as many old cans of the silent movies stored inside as he could, then coat the set with their contents. "Are you mad?" Brooks, a noted rager, raged. "That's the heritage of our craft." The fire marshall shook his head sadly. He knew that. But he also knew that no one had put much thought into how best to preserve it. When Brooks opened those precious cans of ancient history, what he mostly found was highly combustible silver nitrate powder; the old film had decomposed as badly as a forgotten corpse. Brooks spread it around the set, and, as the past exploded around him, a remarkable movie moment rose from its ash. Still, what was lost in those cans remains lost forever.

Thankfully, baseball's past has been better preserved in archives and libraries from coast to coast. But preserving the past isn't enough. These stories aren't just museum pieces; they live with the spirits of their creators and the spirit of the game. Now and again, they need to come out, stretch their muscles, and show off just how good they are. For them. And for us.

In collecting these twenty-two stories, I feel honored by the chance to dust off some deserving old warhorses—familiar ones like "Casey at the Bat," and the deliciously arcane, like Philipine war hero Frederick Funston's 1894 account of baseball in frigid Alaska—insert them into a new lineup, and send them up for another cut. I have no doubt they'll connect—with that part inside every fan that dies a little bit each October only to be reborn again in the spring.

WHY BASE BALL HAS BECOME OUR NATIONAL GAME

ALBERT G. SPALDING

Have we, of America, a National Game? Is there in our country a form of athletic pastime which is distinctively American?

Do our people recognize, among their diversified field sports, one standing apart from every other, outclassing all in its hold upon the interest and affection of the masses? If a negative reply may truthfully be given to all or any of these queries, then this book should never have been published—or written.

But, if we have a National Game; if we know a form of athletics which is peculiarly American, and have adopted it as our own; if it is American in its spirit, its character and its achievements; if it conforms in every way to the American temperament; if we have a field sport outranking all others in popularity, then it is indeed time that the writing, in personal reminiscence, of its story in book form should begin, "lest we forget" the salient points in the inception, evolution and development of so important a factor in the widespread entertainment of the American people and the physical upbuilding of our youth.

To enter upon a deliberate argument to prove that Base Ball is our National Game; that it has all the attributes of American origin,

American character and unbounded public favor in America, seems a work of supererogation. It is to undertake the elucidation of a patent fact; the sober demonstration of an axiom; it is like a solemn declaration that two plus two equal four.

Every citizen of this country who is blessed with organs of vision knows that whenever the elements are favorable and wherever grounds are available, the great American game is in progress, whether in city, village or hamlet, east, west, north or south, and that countless thousands of interested spectators gather daily throughout the season to witness contests which are to determine the comparative excellence of competing local organizations or professional league teams.

The statement will not be successfully challenged that the American game of Base Ball attracts more numerous and larger gatherings of spectators than any other form of field sport in any land. It must also be admitted that it is the only game known for which the general public is willing day after day to pay the price of admission. In exciting political campaigns, Presidential candidates and brilliant orators will attract thousands; but let there be a charge of half a dollar imposed, and only Base Ball can stand the test.

I claim that Base Ball owes its prestige as our National Game to the fact that as no other form of sport it is the exponent of American Courage, Confidence, Combativeness; American Dash, Discipline, Determination; American Energy, Eagerness, Enthusiasm; American Pluck, Persistency, Performance; American Spirit, Sagacity, Success; American Vim, Vigor, Virility.

Base Ball is the American Game *par excellence,* because its playing demands Brain and Brawn, and American manhood supplies these ingredients in quantity sufficient to spread over the entire continent.

No man or boy can win distinction on the ball field who is not, as man or boy, an athlete, possessing all the qualifications which an intelligent, effective playing of the game demands. Having these, he has within him the elements of pronounced success in other walks of life. In demonstration of this broad statement of fact, one needs only to note the brilliant array of statesmen, judges, lawyers, preachers, teachers, engineers, physicians, surgeons, merchants, manufacturers, men of eminence in all the professions and in every avenue of commercial and industrial activity, who have graduated from the ball field to enter upon honorable careers as American citizens of the highest type, each with a sane mind in a sound body.

It seems impossible to write on this branch of the subject—to treat of Base Ball as our National Game—without referring to Cricket, the national field sport of Great Britain and most of her colonies. Every writer on this theme does so. But, in instituting a comparison between these games of the two foremost nations of earth, I must not be misunderstood. Cricket is a splendid game, for Britons. It is a genteel game, a conventional game—and our cousins across the Atlantic are nothing if not conventional. They play Cricket because it accords with the traditions of their country so to do; because it is easy and does not overtax their energy or their thought. They play it because they like it and it is the proper thing to do. Their sires, and grandsires, and great-grandsires played Cricket—why not they? They play Cricket because it is their National Game, and every Briton is a Patriot. They play it persistently—and they play it well. I have played Cricket and like it. There are some features about that game which I admire more than I do some things about Base ball.

But Cricket would never do for Americans; it is too slow. It takes two and sometimes three days to complete a first-class Cricket match; but two hours of Base Ball is quite sufficient to exhaust both players and spectators. An Englishman is so constituted by nature that he can wait three days for the result of a Cricket match; while two hours is about as long as an American can wait for the close of a Base Ball game—or anything else, for that matter. The best Cricket team ever organized in America had its home in Philadelphia—and remained there. Cricket does not satisfy the red-hot blood of Young or Old America.

The genius of our institutions is democratic; Base ball is a democratic game. The spirit of our national life is combative; Base Ball is a combative game. We are a cosmopolitan people, knowing no arbitrary class distinctions, acknowledging none. The son of a President of the United States would as soon play ball with Patsy Flannigan as with Lawrence Lionel Livingstone, provided only that Patsy could put up the right article. Whether Patsy's dad was a banker or boiler-maker would never enter the mind of the White House lad. It would be quite enough for him to know that Patsy was up in the game.

I have declared that Cricket is a genteel game. It is. Our British Cricketer, having finished his day's labor at noon, may don his negligee shirt, his white trousers, his gorgeous hosiery and his canvas shoes, and sally forth to the field of sport, with his sweetheart on one arm and his Cricket bat under the other, knowing that he may engage in his national pastime without soiling his linen or neglecting his lady. He may play Cricket, drink afternoon tea, flirt, gossip, smoke, take a whiskey-and-soda at the customary hour, and have a jolly, conventional good time, don't you know?

Not so the American Ball Player. He may be a veritable Beau Brummel in social life. He may be the Swellest Swell of the Smart Set in Swelldom; but when he dons his Base Ball suit, he says good-bye to society, doffs his gentility, and becomes—just a Ball Player! He knows that his business now is to play ball, and that first of all he is expected to attend to business. It may happen to be his business to slide; hence, forgetting his beautiful new flannel uniform, he cares not if the mud is four inches deep at the base he intends to reach. His sweetheart may be in the grandstand—she probably is—but she is not for him while the game lasts.

Cricket is a gentle pastime. Base Ball is War! Cricket is an Athletic Sociable, played and applauded in a conventional, decorous and English manner.

Base Ball is an Athletic Turmoil, played and applauded in an unconventional, enthusiastic and American manner.

The founder of our National Game became a Major General in the United States Army! The sport had its baptism when our country was in the preliminary agonies of a fratricidal conflict. Its early evolution was among the men, both North and South, who, during the war of the sixties, played the game to relieve the monotony of camp life in those years of melancholy struggle. It was the medium by which, in the days following the "late unpleasantness," a million warriors and their sons, from both belligerent sections, passed naturally, easily, gracefully, from a state of bitter battling to one of perfect peace. Base Ball, I repeat, is War! and the playing of the game is a battle in which every contestant is a commanding General, who, having a field of occupation, must defend it; who, having gained an advantage, must hold it by the employment of every faculty of his brain and body, by every resource of his mind and muscle.

But it is a bloodless battle; and when the struggle ends, the foes of the minute past are friends of the minute present, victims congratulating victors, conquerors pointing out the brilliant individual plays of the conquered.

It would be as impossible for a Briton, who had not breathed the air of this free land as a naturalized American citizen; for one who had no part or heritage in the hopes and achievements of our country, to play Base Ball, as it would for an American, free from the trammels of English traditions, customs, conventionalities, to play the national game of Great Britain.

Let such an Englishman stand at the batter's slab on an American ball field, facing the son of an American President in the pitcher's box, and while he was ruminating upon the propriety of hitting, in his "best form," a ball delivered by the hands of so august a personage, the President's boy would probably shoot three hot ones over the plate, and the Umpire's "Three strikes; you're out," would arouse our British cousin to a realization that we have a game too lively for any but Americans to play.

On the other hand, if one of our cosmopolitan ball artists should visit England, and attempt a game of Cricket, whether it were Cobb, Lajoie, Wagner, or any American batsman of Scandinavian, Irish, French or German antecedents; simply because he was an American, and even though the Cricket ball were to be bowled at his feet by King George himself, he would probably hit the sphere in regular Base Ball style, and smash all conventionalities at the same time, in his eager effort to clear the bases with a three-bagger.

The game of Base Ball is American as to another peculiar feature. It is the only form of field sport known where spectators have an important part and actually participate in the game. Time was, and not long ago, when comparatively few understood the playing rules; but the day has come when nearly every man and boy in the land is versed in all the intricacies of the pastime; thousands of young women have learned it well enough to keep score, and the number of matrons who know the difference between the short-stop and the back-stop is daily increasing.

But neither our wives, our sisters, our daughters, nor our sweethearts, may play Base Ball on the field. They may play Cricket, but seldom do; they may play Lawn Tennis, and win championships; they may play Basket Ball, and achieve laurels; they may play Golf, and receive trophies; but Base Ball is too strenuous for womankind, except as she may take part in grandstand, with applause for the brilliant play, with waving kerchief to the hero of the three-bagger, and, since she is ever a loyal partisan of the home team, with smiles of derision for the Umpire when he gives us the worst of it, and, for the same reason, with occasional perfectly decorous demonstrations when it becomes necessary to rattle the opposing pitcher.

But spectators of the sterner sex may play the game on field, in grandstand or on bleachers, and the influence they exert upon the contest is hardly less than that of the competitors themselves.

In every town, village and city is the local wag. He is a Base Ball fan from infancy. He knows every player in the League by sight and by name. He is a veritable encyclopedia of information on the origin, evolution and history of the game. He can tell you when the Knickerbockers were organized, and knows who led the batting list in every team of the National and American Leagues last year. He never misses a game. His witticisms, ever seasoned with spice, hurled at the visitors and now and then at the Umpire, are as thoroughly enjoyed by all who hear them as is any other feature of the sport. His words of encouragement to the home team, his shouts of derision to the opposing players, find sympathetic responses in the hearts of all present.

But it is neither the applause of the women nor the jokes of the wag which make for victory or defeat in comparison with the work of the "Rooter." He is ever present in large numbers. He is there to see the "boys" win. Nothing else will satisfy him. He is bound by no rules of the game, and too often, perhaps, by no laws of decorum. His sole object in life for two mortal hours is to gain victory for the home team, and that he is not overscrupulous as to the amount of racket emanating from his immediate vicinity need not be emphasized here.

And so it comes to pass that at every important game there is an exhibition in progress, in grandstand and on bleachers, that is quite as interesting in its features of excitement and entertainment as is the contest on the field of sport, and which, in its bearing upon the final result, is sometimes a factor nearly as potent as are the efforts of the contesting players. It must be admitted that as the game of Base Ball has become more generally known; that is, as patrons of the sport are coming to be more familiar with its rules and its requirements, their enjoyment has immeasurably increased; because, just in so far as those in attendance understand the features presented in every play, so far are they able to become participators in the game itself And beyond doubt it is to this growing knowledge on the part of the general public with the pastime that its remarkable popularity is due. For, despite the old adage, familiarity does *not* breed contempt, but fondness, and all America has come to regard Base Ball as its very own, to be known throughout the civilized world as the great American National Game.

Finally, in one other particular Base Ball has won its right to be denominated the American National Game. Ever since its establishment in the hearts of the people as the foremost of field sports, Base Ball has "followed the flag." It followed the flag to the front in the sixties, and received then an impetus which has carried it to half a century of wondrous growth and prosperity. It has followed the flag to Alaska, where, under the midnight sun, it is played on Arctic ice. It has followed the flag to the Hawaiian Islands, and at once supplanted every other form of athletics in popularity. It has followed the flag to the Philippines, to Porto Rico and to Cuba, and wherever a ship floating the Stars and Stripes finds anchorage to-day, somewhere on nearby shore the American National Game is in progress.

THE MODEL BASE BALL PLAYER

BALL PLAYER

HENRY CHADWICK

This is an individual not often seen on a ball ground, but he nevertheless exists, and as a description of his characteristics will prove advantageous, we give a pen photogram of him, in the hope that his example will be followed on all occasions, for if it were, an end would at once be put to many actions which now give rise to unpleasantness on our ball grounds.

HIS MORAL ATTRIBUTES

The principal rule of action of our model base ball player is to comport himself like a gentleman on all occasions, but especially on match days, and in doing so, he abstains from *profanity* and its twin and evil brother obscenity, leaving these vices to be alone cultivated by graduates of our penitentiaries.

He never takes an ungenerous advantage of his opponents, but acts towards them as he would wish them to act towards himself. Regarding the game as a healthful exercise, and a manly and exciting recreation, he plays it solely for the pleasure it affords him, and if victory crowns his efforts in a contest, well and good, but should defeat ensue he is equally ready to applaud the success obtained by his opponents; and by such action he robs defeat of half its sting, and greatly adds to the pleasure the game has afforded both himself and his adversaries.

He never permits himself to be pecuniarily involved in a match, for knowing the injurious tendency of such a course of action to the best interests of the game, he values its welfare too much to make money an object in view in playing ball.

HIS PLAYING QUALIFICATIONS

The physical qualifications of our model player are as follows:

To be able to throw a ball with accuracy of aim a dozen or a hundred yards.

To be fearless in facing and stopping a swiftly batted or thrown ball.

To be able to catch a ball either on the "fly" or bound, either within an inch or two of the ground, or eight or ten feet from it, with either the right or left hand, or both.

To be able to hit a swiftly pitched ball or a bothering slow one, with equal skill, and also to command his bat so as to hit the ball either within six inches of the ground or as high as his shoulder, and either towards the right, centre or left fields, as occasion may require.

To be able to occupy any position on the field creditably, but to *excel in one position* only. To be familiar, practically and theoretically, with every rule of the game and "point" of play.

To conclude our description of a model base ball player, we have to say, that his conduct is as much marked by courtesy of demeanor and liberality of action as it is by excellence in a practical exemplification of the beauties of the game; and his highest aim is to characterize every contest in which he may be engaged, with conduct that will mark it as much as a trial as to which party excels in the moral attributes of the game, as it is one that decides any questions of physical superiority.

CASEY AT THE BAT

ERNEST LAWRENCE THAYER

The outlook wasn't brilliant for the Mudville nine that day;
The score stood four to two with but one inning more to play.
And then when Cooney died at first, and Barrows did the same,
A sickly silence fell upon the patrons of the game.

A straggling few got up to go in deep despair. The rest
Clung to that hope which springs eternal in the human breast;
They thought if only Casey could but get a whack at that—
We'd put up even money now with Casey at the bat.

But Flynn preceded Casey, as did also Jimmy Blake,
And the former was a lulu and the latter was a cake;
So upon that stricken multitude grim melancholy sat,
For there seemed but little chance of Casey's getting to the bat.

But Flynn let drive a single, to the wonderment of all,
And Blake, the much despised, tore the cover off the ball;
And when the dust had lifted, and the men saw what had occurred,
There was Johnnie safe at second and Flynn a-hugging third

Then from 5,000 throats and more there rose a lusty yell;
It rumbled through the valley, it rattled in the dell;
It knocked upon the mountain and recoiled upon the flat,
For Casey, mighty Casey, was advancing to the bat.

There was ease in Casey's manner as he stepped into his place;
There was pride in Casey's bearing and a smile on Casey's face.
And when, responding to the cheers, he lightly doffed his hat,
No stranger in the crowd could doubt 'twas Casey at the bat.

Ten thousand eyes were on him as he rubbed his hands with dirt;
Five thousand tongues applauded when he wiped them on his shirt.
Then while the writhing pitcher ground the ball into his hip,
Defiance gleamed in Casey's eye, a sneer curled Casey's lip.

And now the leather-covered sphere came hurtling through the air,
And Casey stood a-watching it in haughty grandeur there.
Close by the sturdy batsman the ball unheeded sped—
"That ain't my style," said Casey. "Strike one," the umpire said.

From the benches, black with people, there went up a muffled roar.
Like the beating of the storm-waves on a stern and distant shore.
"Kill him; Kill the umpire!" shouted some one on the stand;
And it's likely they'd have killed him had not Casey raised his hand.

With a smile of Christian charity great Casey's visage shone;
He stilled the rising tumult; he bade the game go on;
He signaled to the pitcher, and once more the spheroid flew;
But Casey still ignored it, and the umpire said, "Strike two."

"Fraud!" cried the maddened thousands, and echo answered fraud;
But one scornful look from Casey and the audience was awed.

They saw his face grow stern and cold, they saw his muscles strain,
And they knew that Casey wouldn't let that ball go by again.

The sneer is gone from Casey's lip, his teeth are clenched in hate;
He pounds with cruel violence his bat upon the plate.
And now the pitcher holds the ball, and now he lets it go,
And now the air is shattered by the force of Casey's blow.

Oh, somewhere in this favored land the sun is shining bright;
The band is playing somewhere, and somewhere hearts are light.
And somewhere men are laughing, and somewhere children shout;
But there is no joy in Mudville—mighty Casey has struck out.

CASEY'S REVENGE

GRANTLAND RICE

There were saddened hearts in Mudville for a week or even more;
There were muttered oaths and curses—every fan in town was sore.
"Just think," said one, "How soft it looked with Casey at the bat,
And to think he'd go and spring a bush league trick like that."

All his past fame was forgotten—he was now a hopeless "shine"—
They called him "Strike-out Casey" from the mayor down the line;
And as he came to bat each day his bosom heaved a sigh,
While a look of hopeless fury shone in mighty Casey's eye.

He pondered in the days gone by that he had been their king;
That when he strolled up to the plate they made the welkin ring;
But now his nerve had vanished—for when he heard them hoot,
He "fanned" or "popped out" daily, like some minor league recruit.

He soon began to sulk and loaf—his batting eye went lame;
No home runs on the score card now were chalked against his name;
The fans without exception gave the manager no peace,
For one and all kept clamoring for Casey's quick release.

The Mudville squad began to slump—the team was in the air;
Their playing went from bad to worse—nobody seemed to care;
"Back to the woods with Casey!" was the cry from Rooters' Row—
"Get some one who can hit the ball and let that big dub go!"

The lane is long, some one has said, that never turns again,
And fate, though fickle, often gives another chance to men;
And Casey smiled—his rugged face no longer wore afrown—
Thepitcher who had started all the trouble came to town.

All Mudville had assembled—ten thousand fans had come
To see the twirler who had put big Casey on the bum;
And when he stepped into the box the multitude went wild;
He doffed his cap in proud disdain—but Casey only smiled.

"Play ball!" the umpire's voice rang out—and then the game began;
But in that throng of thousands there was not a single fan
Who thought that Mudville had a chance, and with the setting sun
Their hopes sank low—the rival team was leading, "four to one."

The last half of the ninth came round, with no change in the score,
But when the first man up hit safe the crowd began to roar;
The din increased—the echo of ten thousand shouts was heard
When the pitcher hit the second and gave "four balls" to the third.

Three men on base—nobody out—three runs to tie the game:
A triple meant the highest niche in Mudville's hall of fame;
But here the rally ended and the gloom was deep as night,
When the fourth one "fouled to catcher" and the fifth "flew out to right!"

A dismal groan in chorus came—a scowl was on each face—
When Casey walked up, bat in hand, and slowly took his place;

His bloodshot eyes in fury gleamed—his teeth were clinched in hate,
He gave his cap a vicious hook and pounded on the plate.

But fame is fleeting as the winds and glory fades away;
There were no wild and wooly cheers—no glad acclaim this day;
They hissed and groaned and hooted as they clamored, "Strike him out!"
But Casey gave no outward sign that he had heard this shout.

The pitcher smiled and cut one loose—across the plate it sped—
Another hiss—another groan—"Strike one!" the umpire said.
Zip! Like a shot the second curve broke just below his knee—
"Strike two!" the umpire roared aloud—but Casey made no plea.

No roasting for the umpire now—his was an easy lot;
But here the pitcher whirls again—was that a rifle shot?
A whack—a crack—and out through space the leather pellet flew—
A blot against the distant sky—a speck against the blue.

Above the fence in center field in rapid, whirling flight
The sphere sailed on—the blot grew dim and then was lost to sight,
Ten thousand hats were thrown in air—ten thousand threw a fit—
But no one ever found the ball that mighty Casey hit.

Oh, somewhere in this favored land dark clouds may hide the sun,
And somewhere bands no longer play and children have no fun,
And somewhere over blighted lives there hangs a heavy pall;
But Mudville hearts are happy now—for Casey hit the ball.

THE COLOR LINE

SOL WHITE

In no other profession has the color line been drawn more rigidly than in base ball. As far back as 1872 the first colored ball player of note playing on a white team was Bud Fowler, the celebrated promoter of colored ball clubs, and the sage of base ball. Bud played on a New Castle, Pennsylvania, team that year. Later the Walker Brothers, Fleet and Weldy, played on prominent college teams of the West. Fleet Walker has the distinction of being the only known colored player that ever played iti one of the big leagues. In 1884 Walker caught for Toledo in the old American Association. At this time the Walker brothers and Bud Fowler were the only negroes in the profession.

In 1886 Frank Grant joined Buffalo, of the International League.

In 1887 no less than twenty colored ball players scattered among the different smaller leagues of the country.

With Walker, Grant, Stovy, Fowler, Higgins and Renfro in the International League, White, W. Walker, N. Higgins and R. Johnson in the Ohio League, and others in the West, made 1887 a banner year for colored talent in the white leagues. But this year marked the beginning of the elimination of colored players from white clubs. All the leagues, during the Winter of 1887 and 1888, drew the color line, or had a clause inserted in their constitutions limiting the number of colored players to be employed by each club.

This color line has been agitated by A. C. Anson, Captain of the Chicago National League team for years. As far back as 1883, Anson, with his team, landed in Toledo, O., to play an exhibition game with the American Association team. Walker, the colored catcher, was a member of the Toledos at the time. Anson at first absolutely refused to play his nine against Walker, the colored man, until he was told he could either play with Walker on this team or take his nine off the field. Anson in 1887 again refused to play the Newark Eastern League with Stovey, the colored pitcher, in the box. Were it not for this same man Anson, there would have been a colored player in the National League in 1887. John M. Ward, of the New York club, was anxious to secure Geo. Stovey and arrangements were about completed for his transfer from the Newark club, when a brawl was heard from Chicago to New York. The same Anson, with all the venom of hate which would be worthy of a Tillman or a Vardaman of the present day, made strenuous and fruitful opposition to any proposition looking to the admittance of a colored man into the National League. Just why Adrian C. Anson, manager and captain of the Chicago National League Club, was so strongly opposed to colored players on white teams cannot be explained. His repugnant feeling, shown at every opportunity, toward colored ball players, was a source of comment through every league in the country, and his opposition, with his great popularity and power in base ball circles, hastened the exclusion to the black man from the white leagues.

The colored players are not only barred from playing on white clubs, but at times games are canceled for no other reason than objections being raised by a Southern ball player, who refuses to play against a colored ball club. These men from the South who object to playing are, as a rule, fine ball players, and rather than lose their services, the managers will not book a colored team.

The colored ball player suffers great inconvenience, at times, while traveling. All hotels are generally filled from the cellar to the garret when they strike a town. It is a common occurrence for them to arrive in a city late at night and walk around for several hours before getting a place to lodge.

The situation is far different to-day in this respect than it was years ago. At one time the colored teams were accommodated in some of the best hotels in the country, as the entertainment in 1887 of the Cuban Giants at the McClure House in Wheeling, W. Va., will show.

The cause of this change is no doubt due to the condition of things from a racial standpoint. With the color question upper-most in the minds of the people at the present time, such proceedings on the part of hotel-keepers may be expected and will be difficult to remedy.

It is said on good authority that one of the leading players and a manager of the National League is advocating the entrance of colored players in the National League with a view of signing "Matthews," the colored man, late of Harvard. It is not expected that he will succeed in this advocacy of such a move, but when such actions come to notice there are grounds for hoping that some day the bar will drop and some good man will be chosen from out of the colored profession that will be a credit to all, and pave the way for others to follow.

This article would not be complete did we not mention the effort of John McGraw, manager of the New York National League, to sign a colored man for his Baltimore American League team.

While Manager McGraw was in Hot Springs, Ark., preparing to enter the season of 1901, he was attracted toward Chas. Grant, second baseman of the Columbia Giants of Chicago, who was also at

Hot Springs, playing on a colored team. McGraw, whose knowledge of and capacity for base ball is surpassed by none, thought he saw in Grant a ball player and a card. With the color line so rigidly enforced in the American League, McGraw was at a loss as to how he could get Grant for his Baltimore bunch. The little Napoleon of base ball with a brain for solving intricate circumstances in base ball transactions, conceived the idea of introducing Grant in the league as an Indian. Had it not been for friends of Grant being so eager to show their esteem while the Baltimores were playing in Chicago, McGraw's little scheme would have worked nicely. As it was the bouquet tendered to Grant, which was meant as a gift for the colored man, was really his undoing. McGraw was immediately notified to release Grant at once, as colored players would not be tolerated in the league. This shows what a base ball man will do to get a winner and also shows why McGraw has been called by many, the greatest of all base ball managers.

The following open letter was sent to President McDermit, of the Tri-State (formerly Ohio) League, by Weldy Walker, a member of the Akron, 0., team of 1887, which speaks for itself.

The letter was dated March 5th, 1888. The law prohibiting the employment of colored players in the league was rescinded a few weeks later.

Steubenville, O.,

March 5—Mr. McDermit, President Tri-State League—Sir:

I take the liberty of addressing you because noticing in The Sporting Life that the "law," permitting colored men to sign was repealed, etc., at the special meeting held at Columbus, February 22, of the above-named League of which you are the president. I ascertaining the reason of such an action I have grievances, it is a question with me whether individual loss subserves the public good in this case. This is the only question to be considered—both morally and financially—in this, as it is, or ought to be, in all cases that convinced beyond doubt that you all, as a body of men, have not been impartial and unprejudiced in your consideration of the great and important question—the success of the "National game."

The reason I say this is because you have shown partiality by making an exception with a member of the Zanesville Club, and from this one would infer that he is the only one of the three colored players Dick Johnson, alias Dick Neale, alias Dick Noyle, as the Sporting Life correspondent from Columbus has it; Sol White, of the Wheelings, whom I must compliment by saying was one, if not the surest hitter in the Ohio League last year, and your humble servant, who was unfortunate enough to join the Akron just ten days before they busted.

It is not because I was reserved and have been denied making my bread and butter with some clubs that I speak; but it is in hopes that the action taken at your last meeting will be called up for reconsideration at your next.

The law is a disgrace to the present age, and reflect very much upon the intelligence of your last meeting, and casts derision at the laws of Ohio—the voice of the people—that says all men are equal. I would suggest that your honorable body, in case that black law is not repealed, pass one making it criminal for a colored man or woman to be found in a ball ground.

There is now the same accommodation made for the colored patron of the game as the white, and the same provision and dispensation is made for the money of them both that finds its way into the coffers of the various clubs.

There should be some broader cause—such as lack of ability, behavior and intelligence—for barring a player, rather than his color. It is for these reasons and because I think ability and intelligence should be recognized first and last—at all times and by everyone—I ask the question again why was the "law permitting colored men to sign repealed, etc.?"

Yours truly,

WELDY W. WALKER

A WHALE OF
A PASTIME

BRIG. GEN. FREDERICK FUNSTON

On the 29th day of March, 1894, a party of eleven Tinneh Indians and myself, after a twenty days' snowshoe journey across the bleak tundras and mountain ranges of Northeastern Alaska, reached Herschel Island, in the Arctic Ocean, sixty miles west of the mouth of the Mackenzie River. Here, in a little cove, locked fast in the ice, were the steam whalers Balæna, Grampus, Mary D. Hume, Newport, Narwhal, Jeanette and Karluck, all of San Francisco. Some of these vessels had been out from their home port three years. The preceding October, after one of the most successful seasons in the history of Arctic whaling, all had sought shelter in the only harbor afforded by this desolate coast to lie up for the winter. The ice-packs coming down from the North had frozen in all about Herschel Island, so that as far as the eye could reach was a jumble of bergs and solid floe, but behind the island where the ships lay the salt water had frozen as level as a floor. The nine months that the whalemen were compelled to lie in idleness, while not enlivened by social gayeties, were far from monotonous. With lumber brought up from San Francisco there had been built on shore a commodious one-room house, whose most conspicuous articles of furniture were a big stove that roared day and night, a billiard table and a number of benches and chairs. This was the clubroom of the sixty or seventy officers of the fleet, and here they congregated to play billiards and whist or sit about through the long Arctic evenings, while the wind howled outside, smoking and spinning yarns of many seas, or of boyhood days at New Bedford, New London and Martha's Vineyard. There were veterans who had whaled on every ocean, and had been in nearly every port on the globe; men who recollected well the raid of the cruiser Shenandoah when she burned the fleet on the coast of Siberia thirty years before, and who had been in the Point Barrow disaster, when nearly a score of ships were crushed in the ice floe. The sailors and firemen of the fleet did not have the privileges of this house, but contented themselves with games and amusements of their own. They had an orchestra that played long and vociferously, and there was an amateur dramatic troupe that gave entertainments during the winter. But it was on the great national game of Base Ball that officers and men most depended to break the tedium of their long imprisonment and furnish needed exercise.

A large number of bats and balls had been brought up from San Francisco by one of last summer's arrivals, and as soon as the ships had gone into quarters seven clubs were organized and formed into a league to play for the "Arctic Whalemen's Pennant," which was a strip of drilling nailed to a broomhandle. One nine was composed entirely of officers, another of seamen, a third of firemen, a fourth of cooks and waiters, and so on—the seven nines constituting the "Herschel Island League." A set of written rules provided that the series of games should begin after a month's practice and continue throughout the winter, and that all must be played on schedule time regardless of weather. Another provision was that on the diamond all ship rank was obliterated, and a sailor could "boss" even venerable Capt. Murray without fear of reproof. No sooner had the harbor frozen over than the diamond was laid out and practice begun. Salt water ice is not quite so slippery as that from fresh water, but great care had to be used by the players.

After a season of practice, during which there was much speculation as to the merits of the various nines and no end of chaff and banter, the first game of the series was played, and in the brief twilight of an arctic December day, with the mercury 38° below zero, the "Roaring Gimlets" vanquished the "Pig-Stickers" by a score of 62 to 49. All winter, regardless of blizzards and of bitter cold, the games went on, three or four each week, until the schedule was exhausted, and by this time the rivalry was so intense that playing was continued, the clubs challenging each other indiscriminately. The provision in the bylaws that a club refusing to play on account of weather forfeited its position caused one game to be played at 47° below zero, and often during blizzards the air was so full of flying snow that the outfielders could not be seen from the home-plate. Even after the sun had disappeared for the last time and the long arctic night had begun, games were played in the few hours of twilight at midday, but were usually limited to four innings, as by 2 o'clock it would be too dark to see the ball.

All the whalemen were dressed in the Esquimau fur costume, only the face being exposed, and on their hands wore heavy fur mittens. These clumsy mittens, together with the fact that one was apt to fall on the ice unless he gave a large part of his attention to keeping his feet underneath him, made good catching practically impossible. "Muffs" were the rule, and the man who caught and held the ball received an ovation, not only from the whalers, but from the hundreds of Esquimaux who were always crowded about the rope. With the ball frozen as hard as a rock, no one was apt to repeat an experiment of catching with bare hands. One of the center fielders was a corpulent Orkney Islander, whose favorite method of stopping a hot grounder was to lie down in front of it. The Esquimaux considered him the star player of the fleet. Sliding was the only thing done to perfection, the ice offering excellent facilities for distinction in that line; and there was always a wild cheer when a runner, getting too much headway, knocked the baseman off his feet and both came down together. The scores were ridiculously large, seldom less than fifty on a side, and sometimes twice that. On the smooth ice a good hit meant a home run.

A most amusing feature of the games was the interest shown by the Esquimaux. With the fleet there were nearly a hundred of these people from Behring Strait and Point Barrow, and there were several villages in the vicinity of Herschel Island. These latter were Kogmulliks, the largest Esquimaux in existence, and the presence of the fleet had drawn them from all along the coast. Men, women and children became typical Base Ball cranks, and there was never a game without a large attendance of Esquimaux, who stood about, eyes and mouths wide open, and yelled frantically whenever there was a brilliant catch or a successful slide. At first dozens of them would break over the line and try to hold a runner until the baseman could get the ball, and it was only by vigorous cuffings that they were taught that the spectators' duties are limited to cheering and betting. They borrowed the paraphernalia and tried a few games of their own, but rarely got beyond the first inning, usually winding up in a general melee and hairpulling. One of their umpires, who insisted on allowing a nine to bat after it had three men out in order to even up the score, was dragged off the diamond by his heels. They are naturally great gamblers and bet among themselves on the results of the whalers' games.

A fact that impressed me very much at one of the games that I saw was that the crowd of several hundred people watching our national sport at this faraway corner of the earth, only twenty degrees from the pole, and thousands of miles from railroads or steamship lines, was more widely cosmopolitan than could have been found at any other place on the globe. From the ships were Americans, a hundred or more, men from every seafaring nationality of Europe—Chinese, Japanese and Malays from Tahiti and Hawaii. The colored brother, too, was there, a dozen of him, and several of the players were negroes. Esquimaux of all ages were everywhere, while the red men were represented by the eleven wiry fellows who had snowshoed with me from their home in the valley of the Yukon. One day I noticed that in a little group of eleven, sitting on an overturned sled watching a game, there were representatives of all the five great divisions of the human race.

There are no men on earth who are more hospitable and more thoroughly good fellows than these whalers of the Arctic Ocean, and it was hard to leave them; but we finally got away and started on the long tramp over the snowy wastes toward the Yukon. Just before we left a notice was posted in the clubhouse which, with many "whereases," "aforesaids," and other legal formula, recited that the "Auroras" thought they knew something about ball, and hereby challenged the "Herschels" to meet them on the diamond within three days.

THE RUBE'S HONEYMOON

ZANE GREY

"He's got a new manager. Watch him pitch now!" That was what Nan Brown said to me about Rube Hurtle, my great pitcher, and I took it as her way of announcing her engagement.

My baseball career held some proud moments, but this one, wherein I realized the success of my matchmaking plans, was certainly the proudest one. So, entirely outside of the honest pleasure I got out of the Rube's happiness, there was reason for me to congratulate myself He was a transformed man, so absolutely renewed, so wild with joy, that on the strength of it, I decided the pennant for Worcester was a foregone conclusion, and, sure of the money promised me by the directors, Milly and I began to make plans for the cottage upon the hill.

The Rube insisted on pitching Monday's game against the Torontos, and although poor fielding gave them a couple of runs, they never had a chance. They could not see the ball. The Rube wrapped it around their necks and between their wrists and straight over the plate with such incredible speed that they might just as well have tried to bat rifle bullets.

That night I was happy. Spears, my veteran captain, was one huge smile; Radbourne quietly assured me that all was over now but the shouting; all the boys were happy.

And the Rube was the happiest of all. At the hotel he burst out with his exceeding good fortune. He and Nan were to be married upon the Fourth of July!

After the noisy congratulations were over and the Rube had gone, Spears looked at me and I looked at him.

"Con," said he soberly, "we just can't let him get married on the Fourth."

"Why not? Sure we can. We'll help him get married. I tell you it'll save the pennant for us. Look how he pitched today! Nan Brown is our salvation!" "See here, Con, you've got softenin' of the brain, too. Where's your baseball sense? We've got a pennant to win. By July Fourth we'll be close to the lead again, an' there's that three weeks' trip on the road, the longest an' hardest of the season. We've just got to break even on that trip. You know what that means. If the Rube marries Nan—what are we goin' to do? We can't leave him behind. If he takes Nan with us—why it'll be a honeymoon! An' half the gang is stuck on Nan Brown! An' Nan Brown would flirt in her bridal veil! Why Con, we're up against a worse proposition than ever."

"Good Heavens! Cap. You're right," I groaned. "I never thought of that. We've got to postpone the wedding. . . . How on earth can we? I've heard her tell Milly that. She'll never consent to it. Say, this'll drive me to drink."

"All I got to say is this, Con. If the Rube takes his wife on that trip it's goin' to be an all-fired hummer. Don't you forget that."

"I'm not likely to. But, Spears, the point is this: will the Rube win his games?"

"Figurin' from his work today, I'd gamble he'll never lose another game. It ain't that. I'm thinkin' of what the gang will do to him an' Nan on the cars an' at the hotels. Oh! Lord, Con, it ain't possible to stand for that honeymoon trip! Just think!"

"If the worst comes to the worst, Cap, I don't care for anything but the games. If we get in the lead and stay there I'll stand for anything. . . . Couldn't the gang be coaxed or bought off to let the Rube and Nan alone?"

"Not on your life! There ain't enough love or money on earth to stop them. It'll be awful. Mind, I'm not responsible. Don't you go holdin' me responsible. In all my years of baseball I never went on a trip with a bride in the game. That's new on me, an' I never heard of it. It'd be bad enough if he wasn't a rube an' if she wasn't a crazy girl-fan an' a flirt to boot, an' with half the boys in love with her, but as it is—"

Spears gave up and, gravely shaking his head, he left me. I spent a little while in sober reflection, and finally came to the conclusion that, in my desperate ambition to win the pennant, I would have taken half a dozen rube pitchers and their baseball-made brides on the trip, if by so doing I could increase the percentage of games won. Nevertheless, I wanted to postpone the Rube's wedding if it was possible, and I went out to see Milly and asked her to help us. But for once in her life Milly turned traitor.

"Connie, you don't want to postpone it. Why, how perfectly lovely! Mrs. Stringer will go on that trip and Mrs. Bogart. . . . Connie, I'm going too!"

She actually jumped up and down in glee. That was the woman in her. It takes a wedding to get a woman. I remonstrated and pleaded and commanded, all to no purpose. Milly intended to go on that trip to see the games, and the fun, and the honeymoon.

She coaxed so hard that I yielded. Thereupon she called up Mrs. Stringer on the telephone, and of course found that young woman just as eager as she was. For my part, I threw anxiety and care to the four winds, and decided to ·be as happy as any of them. The pennant was mine! Something kept ringing that in my ears. With the Rube working his iron arm for the edification of his proud Nancy Brown, there was extreme likelihood of divers shutouts and humiliating defeats for some Eastern League teams.

How well I calculated became a matter of baseball history during that last week of June. We won six straight games, three of which fell to the Rube's credit. His opponents scored four runs in the three games, against the nineteen we made. Upon July 1, Radbourne beat Providence and Cairns won the second game. We now had a string of eight victories. Sunday we rested, and Monday was the Fourth, with morning and afternoon games with Buffalo.

Upon the morning of the Fourth, I looked for the Rube at the hotel, but could not find him. He did not show up at the grounds when the other boys did, and I began to worry. It was the Rube's turn to pitch and we were neck and neck with Buffalo for first place. If we won both games we would go ahead of our rivals. So I was all on edge, and kept going to the dressing room to see if the Rube had arrived. He came, finally, when all the boys were dressed, and about to go out for practice. He had on a new suit, a tailor-made suit at that, and he looked fine. There was about him a kind of strange radiance. He stated simply that he had arrived late because he had just been married. Before congratulations were out of our mouths, he turned to me.

"Con, I want to pitch both games today," he said. "What! Say, Whit, Buffalo is on the card today and we are only three points behind them. If we win both we'll be leading the league once more. I don't know about pitching you both games."

"I reckon we'll be in the lead tonight then," he replied, "for I'll win them both."

I was about to reply when Dave, the groundkeeper, called me to the door, saying there was a man to see me. I went out, and there stood Morrisey, manager of the Chicago American League team. We knew each other well and exchanged greetings.

"Con, I dropped off to see you about this new pitcher of yours, the one they call the Rube. I want to see him work. I've heard he's pretty fast. How about it?"

"Wait—till you see him pitch," I replied. I could scarcely get that much out, for Morrisey's presence meant a great deal and I did not want to betray my elation.

"Any strings on him?" queried the big league manager, sharply.

"Well, Morrisey, not exactly. I can give you the first call. You'll have to bid high, though. Just wait till you see him work."

"I'm glad to hear that. My scout was over here watching him pitch and says he's a wonder."

What luck it was that Morrisey should have come upon this day! I could hardly contain myself. Almost I began to spend the money I would get for selling the Rube to the big league manager. We took seats in the grandstand, as Morrisey did not want to be seen by any players, and I stayed there with him until the gong sounded. There was a big attendance. I looked all over the stand for Nan, but she was lost in the gay crowd. But when I went down to the bench I saw her up in my private box with Milly. It took no second glance to see that Nan Brown was a bride and glorying in the fact.

Then, in the absorption of the game, I became oblivious to Milly and Nan; the noisy crowd; the giant firecrackers and the smoke; to the presence of Morrisey; to all except the Rube and my team and their opponents. Fortunately for my hopes, the game opened with characteristic Worcester dash. Little McCall doubled, Ashwell drew his base on four wide pitches, and Stringer drove the ball over the right-field fence—three runs!

Three runs were enough to win that game. Of all the exhibitions of pitching with which the Rube had favored us, this one was the finest. It was perhaps not so much his marvelous speed and unhittable curves that made the game one memorable in the annals of pitching; it was his perfect control in the placing of balls, in the cutting of corners; in his absolute implacable mastery of the situation. Buffalo was unable to find him at all. The game was swift, short, decisive, with the score 5 to 0 in our favor. But the score did not tell all of the Rube's work that morning. He shut out Buffalo without a hit, or a scratch, the first no-hit, no-run game of the year. He gave no base on balls; not a Buffalo player got to first base; only one fly went to the outfield.

For once I forgot Milly after a game, and I hurried to find Morrisey, and carried him off to have dinner with me.

"Your rube is a wonder, and that's a fact," he said to me several times. "Where on earth did you get him? Connelly, he's my meat. Do you understand? Can you let me have him right now?"

"No, Morrisey, I've got the pennant to win first. Then I'll sell him."

"How much? Do you hear? How much?" Morrisey hammered the table with his fist and his eyes gleamed.

Carried away as I was by his vehemence, I was yet able to calculate shrewdly, and I decided to name a very high price, from which I could come down and still make a splendid deal.

"How much?" demanded Morrisey.

"Five thousand dollars," I replied, and gulped when I got the words out.

Morrisey never batted an eye.

"Waiter, quick, pen and ink and paper!"

Presently my hand, none too firm, was signing my name to a contract whereby I was to sell my pitcher for five thousand dollars at the close of the current season. I never saw a man look so pleased as Morrisey when he folded that contract and put it in his pocket. He bade me goodbye and hurried off to catch a train, and he never knew the Rube had pitched the great game on his wedding day.

That afternoon before a crowd that had to be roped off the diamond, I put the Rube against the Bisons. How well he showed the baseball knowledge he had assimilated! He changed his style in that second game. He used a slow ball and wide curves and took things easy. He made Buffalo hit the ball and when runners got on bases once more let out his speed and held them down. He relied upon the players behind him and they were equal to the occasion. It was a totally different game from that of the morning, and perhaps one more suited to the pleasure of the audience. There was plenty of hard hitting, sharp fielding, and good base running, and the game was close and exciting up to the eighth, when Mullaney's triple gave us two runs, and a lead that was not headed. To the deafening roar of the bleachers the Rube walked off the field, having pitched Worcester into first place in the pennant race. That night the boys planned their first job on the Rube. We had ordered a special Pullman for travel to Toronto, and when I got to the depot in the morning, the Pullman was a white fluttering mass of satin ribbons. Also, there was a brass band, and thousands of baseball fans, and barrels of old footgear. The Rube and Nan arrived in a cab and were immediately mobbed. The crowd roared, the band played, the engine whistled, the bell clanged; and the air was full of confetti and slippers, and showers of rice like hail pattered everywhere. A somewhat disheveled bride and groom boarded the Pullman and breathlessly hid in a stateroom. The train started, and the crowd gave one last rousing cheer. Old Spears yelled from the back platform:

"Fellers, an' fans, you needn't worry none about leavin' the Rube an' his bride to the tender mercies of the gang. A hundred years from now people will talk about this honeymoon baseball trip. Wait till we come back—an' say, jest to put you wise, no matter what else happens, we're comin' back in first place!" It was surely a merry party in that Pullman. The bridal couple emerged from their hiding place and held a sort of reception in which the Rube appeared shy and frightened, and Nan resembled a joyous, fluttering bird in gray. I did not see if she kissed every man on the team, but she kissed me as if she had been wanting to do it for ages. Milly kissed the Rube, and so did the other women, to his infinite embarrassment. Nan's effect upon that crowd was most singular. She was sweetness and caprice and joy personified.

We settled down presently to something approaching order, and I, for one, with very keen ears and alert eyes, because I did not want to miss anything.

"I see the lambs a-gambolin'," observed McCall, in a voice louder than was necessary to convey his meaning to Mullaney, his partner in the seat.

"Yes, it do seem as if there was joy a boundin' hereabouts," replied Mul with fervor.

"It's more springtime than summer," said Ashwell, "an' everything in nature is runnin' in pairs. There are the sheep an' the cattle an' the birds. I see two kingfishers fishin' over here. An' there's a couple of honeybees makin' honey. Oh, honey, an' by George, if there ain't two butterflies foldin' their wings round each other. See the dandelions kissin' in the field!"

Then the staid Captain Spears spoke up with an appearance of sincerity and a tone that was nothing short of remarkable.

"Reggie, see the sunshine asleep upon yon bank. Ain't it lovely? An' that white cloud sailin' thither amid the blue—how spontaneous! Joy is abroad o'er all this boo-tiful land today—Oh, yes! An' love's wings hover o'er the little lambs an' the bullfrogs in the pond an' the dicky birds in the trees. What sweetness to lie in the grass, the lap of boun- teous earth, eatin' apples in the Garden of Eden, an' chasin' away the snakes an' dreamin' of Thee, Sweeth-e-a-r-t—"

Spears was singing when he got so far and there was no telling what he might have done if Mullaney, unable to stand the agony, had not jabbed a pin in him. But that only made way for the efforts of the other boys, each of whom tried to outdo the other in poking fun at the Rube and Nan. The big pitcher was too gloriously happy to note much of what went on around him, but when it dawned upon him he grew red and white by turns.

Nan, however, was more than equal to the occasion. Presently she smiled at Spears, such a smile! The captain looked as if he had just par- taken of an intoxicating wine. With a heightened color in her cheeks and a dangerous flash in her roguish eyes, Nan favored McCall with a look, which was as much as to say that she remembered him with a dear sadness. She made eyes at every fellow in the car, and then bring- ing back her gaze to the Rube, as if glorying in comparison, she nes- tled her curly black head on his shoulder. He gently tried to move her; but it was not possible. Nan knew how to meet the ridicule of half a dozen old lovers. One by one they buried themselves in newspapers, and finally McCall, for once utterly beaten, showed a white feather, and sank back out of sight behind his seat.

The boys did not recover from that shock until late in the after- noon. As it was a physical impossibility for Nan to rest her head all day upon her husband's broad shoulder, the boys toward dinnertime came out of their jealous trance. I heard them plotting something. When dinner was called, about half of my party, including the bride and groom, went at once into the dining car. Time there flew by swiftly.

And later, when we were once more in our Pullman, and I had gotten interested in a game of cards with Milly and Stringer and his wife, the Rube came marching up to me with a very red face.

"Con, I reckon some of the boys have stolen my—our grips," said he.

"What?" I asked, blankly.

He explained that during his absence in the dining car someone had entered his stateroom and stolen his grip and Nan's. I hastened at once to aid the Rube in his search. The boys swore by everything under and beyond the sun they had not seen the grips; they appeared very much grieved at the loss and pretended to help in searching the Pullman. At last, with the assistance of a porter, we discovered the missing grips in an upper berth. The Rube carried them off to his stateroom and we knew soon from his uncomplimentary remarks that the contents of the suitcases had been mixed and manhandled. But he did not hunt for the jokers.

We arrived at Toronto before daylight next morning, and remained in the Pullman until seven o'clock. When we got out, it was discovered that the Rube and Nan had stolen a march upon us. We traced them to the hotel, and found them at breakfast. After breakfast we formed a merry sightseeing party and rode all over the city.

That afternoon, when Raddy let Toronto down with three hits and the boys played a magnificent game behind him, and we won 7 to 2, I knew at last and for certain that the Worcester team had come into its own again. Then next day Cairns won a close, exciting game, and following that, on the third day, the matchless Rube toyed with the Torontos. Eleven straight games won! I was in the clouds, and never had I seen so beautiful a light as shone in Milly's eyes.

From that day The Honeymoon Trip of the Worcester Baseball Club, as the newspapers heralded it—was a triumphant march. We won two out of three games at Montreal, broke even with the hard-fighting Bisons, took three straight from Rochester, and won one and tied one out of three with Hartford. It would have been wonderful ball playing for a team to play on home grounds and we were doing the full circuit of the league.

Spears had called the turn when he said the trip would be a hummer. Nan Hurtle had brought us wonderful luck.

But the tricks they played on Whit and his girl-fan bride!

Ashwell, who was a capital actor, disguised himself as a conductor and pretended to try to eject Whit and Nan from the train, urging that lovemaking was not permitted. Some of the team hired a clever young woman to hunt the Rube up at the hotel, and claim old acquaintance with him. Poor Whit almost collapsed when the young woman threw her arms about his neck just as Nan entered the parlor. Upon the instant Nan became wild as a little tigress, and it took much explanation and eloquence to reinstate Whit in her affections.

Another time Spears, the wily old fox, succeeded in detaining Nan on the way to the station, and the two missed the train. At first the Rube laughed with the others, but when Stringer remarked that he had noticed a growing attachment between Nan and Spears, my great pitcher experienced the first pangs of the green-eyed monster. We had to hold him to keep him from jumping from the train, and it took Milly and Mrs. Stringer to soothe him. I had to wire back to Rochester for a special train for Spears and Nan, and even then we had to play half a game without the services of our captain.

So far upon our trip I had been fortunate in securing comfortable rooms and the best of transportation for my party. At Hartford, however, I encountered difficulties. I could not get a special Pullman, and the sleeper we entered already had a number of occupants. After the ladies of my party had been assigned to berths, it was necessary for some of the boys to sleep double in upper berths.

It was late when we got aboard, the berths were already made up, and soon we had all retired. In the morning very early I was awakened by a disturbance. It sounded like a squeal. I heard an astonished exclamation, another squeal, the pattering of little feet, then hoarse uproar of laughter from the ball players in the upper berths. Following that came low, excited conversation between the porter and somebody, then an angry snort from the Rube and the thud of his heavy feet in the aisle. What took place after that was guesswork for me. But I gathered from the roars and bawls that the Rube was after some of the boys. I poked my head between the curtains and saw him digging into the berths.

"Where's McCall?" he yelled.

Mac was nowhere in that sleeper, judging from the vehement denials. But the Rube kept on digging and prodding in the upper berths.

"I'm a-goin' to lick you, Mac, so I reckon you'd better show up," shouted the Rube.

The big fellow was mad as a hornet. When he got to me he grasped me with his great fence-rail splitting hands and I cried out with pain.

"Say! Whit, let up! Mac's not here. . . . What's wrong?"

"I'll show you when I find him." And the Rube stalked on down the aisle, a tragically comic figure in his pajamas. In his search for Mac he pried into several upper berths that contained occupants who were not ball players, and these protested in affright. Then the Rube began to investigate the lower berths. A row of heads protruded in a bobbing line from between the curtains of the upper berths.

"Here, you Indian! Don't you look in there! That's my wife's berth!" yelled Stringer.

Bogart, too, evinced great excitement.

"Hurtle, keep out of lower eight or I'll kill you," he shouted.

What the Rube might have done there was no telling, but as he grasped a curtain, he was interrupted by a shriek from some woman assuredly not of our party.

"Get out! you horrid wretch! Help! Porter! Help! Conductor!"

Instantly there was a deafening tumult in the car. When it had subsided somewhat, and I considered I would be safe, I descended from my berth and made my way to the dressing room. Sprawled over the leather seat was the Rube pommelling McCall with hearty goodwill. I would have interfered, had it not been for Mac's demeanor. He was half frightened, half angry, and utterly unable to defend himself or even resist, because he was laughing, too.

"Doggone it! Whit—I didn't—do it! I swear it was Spears! Stop thumpin' me now—or I'll get sore. . . . You hear me! It wasn't me, I tell you. Cheese it!"

For all his protesting Mac received a good thumping, and I doubted not in the least that he deserved it. The wonder of the affair, however, was the fact that no one appeared to know what had made the Rube so furious. The porter would not tell, and Mac was strangely reticent, though his smile was one to make a fellow exceedingly sure something out of the ordinary had befallen. It was not until I was having breakfast in Providence that I learned the true cause of Rube's conduct, and Milly confided it to me, insisting on strict confidence.

"I promised not to tell," she said. "Now you promise you'll never tell."

"Well, Connie," went on Milly, when I had promised, "it was the funniest thing yet, but it was horrid of McCall. You see, the· Rube had upper seven and Nan had lower seven. Early this morning, about daylight, Nan awoke very thirsty and got up to get a drink. During her absence, probably, but anyway sometime last night, McCall changed the number on her curtain, and when Nan came back to number seven of course she almost got in the wrong berth."

"No wonder the Rube punched him!" I declared. "I wish we were safe home. Something'll happen yet on this trip."

I was faithful to my promise to Milly, but the secret leaked out somewhere; perhaps Mac told it, and before the game that day all the players knew it. The Rube, having recovered his good humor, minded it not in the least. He could not have felt ill will for any length of time. Everything seemed to get back into smooth running order, and the Honeymoon Trip bade fair to wind up beautifully.

But, somehow or other, and about something unknown to the rest of us, the Rube and Nan quarreled. It was their first quarrel. Milly and I tried to patch it up but failed.

We lost the first game to Providence and won the second. The next day, a Saturday, was the last game of the trip, and it was Rube's turn to pitch. Several times during the first two days the Rube and Nan about half made up their quarrel, only in the end to fall deeper into it. Then the last straw came in a foolish move on the part of wilful Nan. She happened to meet Henderson, her former admirer, and in a flash she took up her flirtation with him where she had left off.

"Don't go to the game with him, Nan," I pleaded. "It's a silly thing for you to do. Of course you don't mean anything, except to torment Whit. But cut it out. The gang will make him miserable and we'll lose the game. There's no telling what might happen."

"I'm supremely indifferent to what happens," she replied, with a rebellious toss of her black head. "I hope Whit gets beaten."

She went to the game with Henderson and sat in the grandstand, and the boys spied them out and told the Rube. He did not believe it at first, but finally saw them, looked deeply hurt and offended, and then grew angry. But the gong, sounding at that moment, drew his attention to his business of the day, to pitch.

His work that day reminded me of the first game he ever pitched for me, upon which occasion Captain Spears got the best out of him by making him angry. For several innings Providence was helpless before his delivery. Then something happened that showed me a crisis was near. A wag of a fan yelled from the bleachers.

"Honeymoon Rube!"

This cry was taken up by the delighted fans and it rolled around the field. But the Rube pitched on, harder than ever. Then the knowing bleacherite who had started the cry changed it somewhat.

"Nanny's Rube!" he yelled.

This, too, went the rounds, and still the Rube, though red in the face, preserved his temper and his pitching control. All would have been well if Bud Wiler, comedian of the Providence team, had not hit upon a way to rattle Rube.

"Nanny's Goat!" he shouted from the coaching lines. Every Providence player took it up.

The Rube was not proof against that. He yelled so fiercely at them, and glared so furiously, and towered so formidably, that they ceased for the moment. Then he let drive with his fast straight ball and hit the first Providence batter in the ribs. His comrades had to help him to the bench. The Rube hit the next batter on the leg, and judging from the crack of the ball, I fancied that player would walk lame for several days. The Rube tried to hit the next batter and sent him to first on balls. Thereafter it became a dodging contest with honors about equal between pitcher and batters. The Providence players stormed and the bleachers roared. But I would not take the Rube out and the game went on with the Rube forcing in runs.

With the score a tie, and three men on bases one of the players on the bench again yelled: "Nanny's Goat!"

Straight as a string the Rube shot the ball at this fellow and bounded after it. The crowd rose in an uproar. The base runners began to score. I left my bench and ran across the space, but not in time to catch the Rube. I saw him hit two or three of the Providence men. Then the policemen got to him, and a real fight brought the big audience into the stamping melee. Before the Rube was collared I saw at least four blue-coats on the grass.

The game broke up, and the crowd spilled itself in streams over the field. Excitement ran high. I tried to force my way into the mass to get at the Rube and the officers, but this was impossible. I feared the Rube would be taken from the officers and treated with violence, so I waited with the surging crowd, endeavoring to get nearer. Soon we were in the street, and it seemed as if all the stands had emptied their yelling occupants.

A trolley car came along down the street, splitting the mass of people and driving them back. A dozen policemen summarily bundled the Rube upon the rear end of the car. Some of these officers boarded the car, and some remained in the street to beat off the vengeful fans.

I saw someone thrust forward a frantic young woman. The officers stopped her, then suddenly helped her on the car, just as I started. I recognized Nan. She gripped the Rube with both hands and turned a white, fearful face upon the angry crowd.

The Rube stood in the grasp of his wife and the policemen, and he looked like a ruffied lion. He shook his big fist and bawled in far-reaching voice:

"I can lick you all!"

To my infinite relief, the trolley gathered momentum and safely passed out of danger. The last thing I made out was Nan pressing close to the Rube's side. That moment saw their reconciliation and my joy that it was the end of the Rube's Honeymoon.

HOW I PITCHED
THE FIRST CURVE

CANDY CUMMINGS

I have been asked how I first got the idea of making a ball curve. I will now explain. It is such a simple matter, though, that there is not much explanation.

In the summer of 1863 a number of boys and myself were amusing ourselves by throwing clam shells (the hard-shell variety) and watching them sail along through the air, turning now to the right and now to the left. We became interested in the mechanics of it and experimented for an hour or more.

All of a sudden it came to me that it would be a good joke on the boys if I could make a baseball curve the same way. We had been playing "three old cat" and town ball, and I had been doing the pitching. The joke seemed so good that I made a firm decision that I would try to play it.

I set to work on my theory and practiced every spare moment that I had out of school. I had no one to help me and had to fight it out alone. Time after time I would throw the ball, doubling up into all manner of positions, for I thought that my pose had something to do with it; and then I tried holding the ball in different shapes. Sometimes

I thought I had it, and then maybe again in twenty-five tries I could not get the slightest curve. My visionary successes were just enough to tantalize me. Month after month I kept pegging away at my theory.

In 1864 I went to Fulton, New York, to a boarding school and remained there a year and a half. All that time I kept experimenting with my curve ball. My boyfriends began to laugh at me and to throw jokes at my theory of making a ball go sideways. I fear that some of them thought it was so preposterous that it was no joke and that I should be carefully watched over.

I don't know what made me stick at it. The great wonder to me now is that I did not give up in disgust, for I had not one single word of encouragement in all that time, while my attempts were a standing joke among my friends.

After graduating, I went back to my home in Brooklyn, New York, and joined the "Star Juniors," an amateur team. We were very successful. I was solicited to join as a junior member the Excelsior club, and I accepted the proposition.

In 1867 I, with the Excelsior club, went to Boston, where we played the Lowells, the Tri-Mountains, and Harvard clubs. During these games I kept trying to make the ball curve. It was during the Harvard game that I became fully convinced that I had succeeded in doing what all these years I had been striving to do. The batters were missing a lot of balls; I began to watch the flight of the ball through the air and distinctly saw it curve.

A surge of joy flooded over me that I shall never forget. I felt like shouting out that I had made a ball curve; I wanted to tell everybody; it was too good to keep to myself.

But I said not a word and saw many a batter at that game throw down his stick in disgust. Every time I was successful, I could scarcely keep from dancing from pure joy. The secret was mine.

There was trouble, though, for I could not make it curve when I wanted to. I would grasp it the same, but the ball seemed to do just as it pleased. It would curve, all right, but it was very erratic in its choice of places to do so. But still it curved!

The baseball came to have a new meaning to me; it almost seemed to have life.

It took time and hard work for me to master it, but I kept on pegging away until I had fairly good control.

In those days the pitcher's box was 6 feet by 4, and the ball could be thrown from any part of it; one foot could be at the forward edge of the box, while the other could be stretched back as far as the pitcher liked; but both feet had to be on the ground until the ball was delivered. It is surprising how much speed could be generated under those rules.

It was customary to swing the arm perpendicularly and to deliver the ball at the height of the knee. I still threw this way but brought in wrist action.

I found that the wind had a whole lot to do with the ball curving. With a wind against me I could get all kinds of a curve, but the trouble lay in the fact that the ball was apt not to break until it was past the batter. This was a sore trouble; but I learned not to try to curve a ball very much when the wind was unfavorable.

I have often been asked to give my theory of why a ball curves. Here it is: I give the ball a sharp twist with the middle finger, which causes it to revolve with a swift rotary motion. The air also, for a limited space around it begins to revolve, making a great swirl, until there is enough pressure to force the ball out of true line. When I first began practicing this new legerdemain, the pitchers were not the only ones who were fooled by the ball. The umpire also suffered. I would throw the ball straight at the batter; he would jump back, and then the umpire would call a ball. On this I lost, but when I started the spheroid toward the center of the plate, he would call it a strike. When it got to the batter, it was too far out, and the batter would not even swing. Then there would be a clash between the umpire and the batter. But my idlest dreams of what a curved ball would do as I dreamed of them that afternoon while throwing clam shells have been filled more than a hundred times. At that time I thought of it only as a good way to fool the boys, its real practical significance never entering my mind.

I get a great deal of pleasure now in my old age out of going to games and watching the curves, thinking that it was through my blind efforts that all this was made possible.

DISCOVERING
CY YOUNG

ALFRED H. SPINK

Cy Young, the veteran pitcher, began his career in Cleveland, and Stanley Robison late president of the St. Louis National League Club, was the man who discovered Young. At the time Robison was owner of the Cleveland franchise, and the Spiders, under Pat Tebeau, were large grapes in the major league vineyard.

It happened that Patsy Tebeau was short on pitchers way back about 1893. In those day they did not have scouts combing the country for talent, and the "tipsters" on blooming talent were usually commercial travelers.

Robison was at the time looking over some of his railroad property at Fort Wayne, Ind., and he was lapping up a few "elixirs of mirth," when he happened to open up his vocal chords on baseball. There was a commercial traveler at the bar, who liked baseball, to say nothing of having a fondness for the "elixir" stuff.

Stanley invited him to have a jolt, and also to discuss baseball. "Rather odd," remarked Robison, "that it is so hard to get a good baseball pitcher nowadays. I'm looking for a man for my Cleveland club. I've offered enough real money to choke a manhole to get a fellow from one of the other clubs; but, say, I can't make the deal."

"Have another, and I'll give you the best little three-star special you've ever heard tell of since they named you after Matt Quay," returned the commercial traveler.

After the commercial traveler and M. Stanley had inhaled their mirth water the man of satchels and grips opened the conversation.

"Say, old sport," said the commercial traveler, "you're looking for a pitcher. As I understand the vernacular, you are in quest of someone who can hurl an elusive leather-covered sphere, guaranteed to weigh in ringside at five ounces, and to be of 9-inch circumference, no more or no less, somewhere near a little disk they foolishly refer to as the home plate. Get me?

"Now, my friend, take my tip, pack your grip and go up to Canton. They've got a big kid up there that can do anything with a baseball except eat it. Say, he's got so much speed that he burns chunks of holes in the atmosphere. He's the shoot-'em-in-Pete of that reservation.

"Watched him streak 'em over last Sunday, and he struck out a flock of baseball players. I think he fanned a hundred or two hundred. I didn't keep count. He made them describe figure 'eights,' stand on their beams and wigwag for help. You get your grip, if you want a pitcher, streak it to Canton, and don't let anyone tout you off."

Robison did as he was bade, and when he arrived at Canton he went out to the ball yard. There was a big, lop-sided yap on the mound. He looked as though nature chiseled him out to pitch hay, instead of a poor, little inoffensive baseball, and Robison had to laugh when he beheld the world-renowned bearcat twirler that his friend had tipped him off to. The big boy in the box showed a lot of steam, and Robison's desire to laugh was turned to amazement. He'd never beheld anyone toss a ball with just such speed and precision and with so many curlicues on it. After the game Robison called the young hay miner aside and offered him a job at a figure which made the youth open his mouth.

Robison slipped him transportation to Cleveland, with instructions to find his way out to the ball yard and call on Pat Tebeau, admonishing him to be careful not to get run over by any street cars, as he (Robison) owned the lines and didn't want any damage suits.

The lop-sided boy found his way to the ball yard, asked for Mr. Teabow, blushed like a June bride and told him what he came for.

Tebeau called Zimmer and a few of his old scouts about him, and they openly laughed at the unusual looking boy, who had the nerve to say that he might be a baseball pitcher fit for major league company.

Chicago was in Cleveland. Old fans will recall those dreaded White Stockings, with Anson at their head; and such stars as Ned Williamson, Tommy Burns, Fred Pfeffer, Dalrymple, Jimmy Ryan and that sort on the roster.

Those old boys used to give great pitchers that earthquake feeling about the knees when they dragged up their hundred-pound batons to thump the bitumen out of anything that came near the plate.

Tebeau thought it would be a good joke to pitch the young man against these sluggers and see the effect. He told the boy he wanted him to pitch. Then they dug up a uniform that fitted the lad like a 14½ collar would incase the neck of Frank Gotch.

Anson and his bunch were as fierce baseball pirates as ever scuttled a ship, but they had to laugh at the lad who was to aim the pill at them. They roared when they saw him go into the box.

But something happened. The mere boy struck out Adrian C. Anson, world's wonder with the bat; then he fanned Fred Pfeffer, the prince of second sackers, and slipped three across that Williamson missed entirely.

Then those Chicago sluggers began to take notice. Pat Tebeau saw that the boy he mistook for a clown was a real jewel in the rough. The boy won that game. He made the White Stockings look like a young simian trying to shave. That night the young lad's name was on every tongue. He was Cy Young, farmer, who became a famous baseball pitcher in one day, and who has been making good ever since.

Young is a farmer yet. He cultivates his broad acres in Ohio and is well off.

VARSITY FRANK

BURT L. STANDISH

A day or two later came the very thing that had been anticipated and discussed, since the freshman game at Cambridge. Merriwell was selected as one of the pitchers on the 'Varsity nine, and the freshmen lost him from their team. Putnam came out frankly and confessed that he had feared something of the kind, all along, and Frank was in no mood to kick over his past treatment, so nothing was said on that point.

In the first game against a weaker team than Harvard, Merriwell was tried in the box and pitched a superb game, which Yale won in a walk.

Big Hugh Heffner, the regular pitcher, whose arm was in a bad way, complimented Merriwell on his work, which he said was "simply great."

Of course Frank felt well, as for him there was no sport he admired so much as baseball; but he remained the same old Merriwell, and his freshmen comrades could not see the least change in his manner.

The second game of the series with Harvard came off within a week, but Frank got cold in his arm, and he was not in the best possible condition to go into the box. This he told Pierson, and as Heffner had almost entirely recovered, Frank was left on the bench.

The 'Varsity team had another pitcher, who was known as Dad Hicks. He was a man about twenty-eight years old, and looked even older, hence the nickname of Dad.

This man was most erratic and could not be relied upon. Sometimes he would do brilliant work, and at other time children could have batted him all over the lot. He was used only in desperate emergencies, and could not be counted on in a pinch.

During the whole of the second game with Harvard Frank sat on the bench, ready to go into the box if called on. At first it looked as if he would have to go in, for the Harvard boys fell upon Heffiner and pounded him severely for two innings. Then Hugh braced up and pitched the game through to the end in brilliant style, Yale winning by a score of ten to seven.

Heffiner, however, was forced to bathe his arm in witch hazel frequently, and as he went toward the box for the last time he said to Frank with a rueful smile:

"You'll have to get into shape to pitch the last game of the series with these chaps. My arm is the same as gone now, and I'll finish it this inning. We must win this game anyway, regardless of arms, so here goes."

He could barely get the balls over the plate, but he used his head in a wonderful manner, and the slow ball proved a complete puzzle for Harvard after they had been batting speed all through the game, so they got but one safe hit off Heffiner that inning and no scores.

There was a wild jubilee at Yale that night. A bonfire was built on the campus, and the students blew horns, sang songs, cheered for "good old Yale," and had a real lively time.

One or two of the envious ones asked about Merriwell—why he was not allowed to pitch. Even Hartwick, a sophomore who had disliked Frank from the first, more than hinted that the freshman pitcher was being made sport of, and that he would not be allowed to go into the box when Yale was playing a team of any consequence.

Jack Diamond overheard the remark, and he promptly offered to bet Hartwick any sum that Merriwell would pitch the next game against Harvard.

Diamond was a freshman, and so he received a calling down from Hartwick, who told him he was altogether too new. But as Hartwick strolled away, Diamond quietly said:

"I may be new, sir, but I back up any talk I make. There are others who do not, sir."

Hartwick made no reply.

As the third and final game of the series was to be played on neutral ground, there had been some disagreement about the location, but Springfield had finally been decided upon, and accepted by Yale and Harvard.

Frank did his best to keep his arm in good condition for that game, something which Pierson approved. Hicks was used as much as possible in all other games, but Frank found it necessary to pull one or two off the coals for him.

Heffiner had indeed used his arm up in the grand struggle to win the second game from Harvard—the game that it was absolutely necessary for Yale to secure. He tended that arm as if it were a baby, but it had been strained severely and it came into shape very slowly. As soon as possible he tried to do a little throwing every day, but it was some time before he could get a ball more than ten or fifteen feet.

It became generally known that Merriwell would have to pitch at Springfield, beyond a doubt, and the greatest anxiety was felt at Yale. Every man had confidence in Heffiner, but it was believed by the majority that the freshman was still raw, and therefore was liable to make a wretched fizzle of it.

Heffiner did not think so. He coached Merriwell almost every day, and his confidence in Frank increased.

"The boy is all right," was all he would say about it, but that did not satisfy the anxious ones.

During the week before the deciding game was to come off Heffiner's arm improved more rapidly than it had at any time before, and scores of men urged Pierson to put Old Reliable, as Hugh was sometimes called, into the box.

A big crowd went up to Springfield on the day of the great game, but the "sons of Old Eli" were far from confident, although they were determined to root for their team to the last gasp.

The most disquieting rumors had been afloat concerning Harvard. It was said her team was in a third better condition than at the opening of the season, when she took the first game from Yale; and it could not be claimed with honesty that the Yale team was apparently in any better shape. Although she had won the second game of the series with Harvard, her progress had not been satisfactory.

A monster crowd had gathered to witness the deciding game. Blue and crimson were the prevailing colors. On the bleachers at one side of the grandstand sat hundreds upon hundreds of Harvard men, cheering all together and being answered by the hundreds of Yale men on the other side of the grand stand. There were plenty of ladies and citizens present and the scene was inspiring. A band of music served to quicken the blood in the veins which were already throbbing.

There was short preliminary practice, and then at exactly three o'clock the umpire walked down behind the home plate and called: "Play ball!"

Yale took the field, and as the boys in blue trotted out, the familiar Yale yell broke from hundreds of throats. Blue pennants were wildly fluttering, the band was playing a lively air, and for the moment it seemed as if the sympathy of the majority of the spectators was with Yale.

But when Hinkley, Harvard's great single hitter, who always headed the batting list, walked out with his pet "wagon tongue," a different sound swept over the multitude, and the air seemed filled with crimson pennants.

Merriwell went into the box, and the umpire broke open a pasteboard box, brought out a ball that was wrapped in tin foil, removed the covering, and tossed the snowy sphere to the freshman pitcher Yale had so audaciously stacked up against Harvard.

Frank looked the box over, examined the rubber plate, and seemed to make himself familiar with every inch of the ground in his vicinity. Then he faced Hinkley, and a moment later delivered the first ball.

Hinkley smashed it on the nose, and it was past Merriwell in a second, skipping along the ground and passing over second base just beyond the baseman's reach, although he made a good run for it.

The center fielder secured the ball and returned it to second, but Hinkley had made a safe single off the very first ball delivered.

Harvard roared, while the Yale crowd was silent. A great mob of freshmen was up from New Haven to see the game and watch Merriwell's work, and some of them immediately expressed disappointment and dismay.

"Here is where Merriwell meets his Waterloo," said Sport Harris. "He'll be batted out before the game is fairly begun."

That was quite enough to arouse Rattleton, who heard the remark.

"I'll bet you ten dollars he isn't batted out at all," spluttered Harry, fiercely. "Here's my money, too!"

"Make it twenty-five and I will go you," drawled Harris.

"All right, I'll make it twenty-five."

The money was staked.

Derry, also a heavy hitter, was second on Harvard's list. Derry had a bat that was as long and as large as the regulations would permit, and as heavy as lead; yet, despite the weight of the stick, the strapping Vermonter handled it as if it were a feather.

Frank sent up a coaxer, but Derry refused to be coaxed. The second ball was high, but Derry cracked it for two bags, and Hinkley got around to third.

It began to seem as if Merriwell would be batted out in the first inning, and the Yale crowd looked weary and disgusted at the start.

The next batter fouled out, however, and the next one sent a red-hot liner directly at Merriwell. There was no time to get out of the way, so Frank caught it, snapped the ball to third, found Hinkley off the bag, and retired the side without a score.

This termination of the first half of the inning was so swift and unexpected that it took some seconds for the spectators to realize what had happened. When they did, however, Yale was wildly cheered.

"What do you think about it now, Harris?" demanded Harry, exultantly.

"I think Merriwell saved his neck by a dead lucky catch," was the answer. "If he had missed that ball he would have been removed within five minutes."

Pierson, who was sitting on the bench, was looking doubtful, and he held a consultation with Costigan, captain of the team, as soon as the latter came in from third base.

Costigan asked Frank how he felt, and Merriwell replied that he had never felt better in his life, so it was decided to let him see what he could do in the box the next inning.

Yedding, who was in the box for Harvard, could not have been in better condition, and the first three Yale men to face him went out in one-two-three order, making the first inning a whitewash for both sides.

As Merriwell went into the box the second time there were cries for Heffiner, who was on the bench, ready to pitch if forced to do so, for all of the fact that it might ruin his arm forever, so far as ball playing was concerned.

In trying to deceive the first man up Merriwell gave him three balls in succession. Then he was forced to put them over. He knew the batter would take one or two, and so he sent two straight, swift ones directly over, and two strikes were called.

Then came the critical moment, for the next ball pitched would settle the matter. Frank sent in a rise and the batter struck at it, missed it, and was declared out, the ball having landed with a "plunk" in the hands of the catcher.

The next batter got first on a single, but the third man sent an easy one to Frank, who gathered it in, threw the runner out at second, and the second baseman sent the ball to first in time to retire the side on a double play.

"You are all right, Merriwell, old man," enthusiastically declared Heffiner, as Frank came in to the bench. "They haven't been able to score off you yet, and they won't be able to touch you at all after you get into gear."

Pierson was relieved, and Costigan looked well satisfied.

"Now we must have some scores, boys," said the captain.

But Yedding showed that he was out for blood, for he allowed but one safe hit, and again retired Yale without a score.

Surely it was a hot game, and excitement was running high. Would Harvard be able to score the next time? That was the question everybody was asking.

Yedding came to the bat in this inning, and Merriwell struck him out with ease, while not another man got a safe hit, although one got first on the shortstop's error.

The Yale crowd cheered like Indians when Harvard was shut out for the third time, the freshmen seeming to yell louder than all the others. They originated a cry which was like this:

"He is doing very well! Who? Why, Merriwell!"

Merriwell was the first man up, and Yedding did his best to get square by striking the freshman out. In this he was successful, much to his satisfaction.

But no man got a hit, and the third inning ended as had the others, neither side having made a run.

The fourth opened in breathless suspense, but it was quickly over, neither side getting a man beyond second.

It did not seem possible that this thing could continue much longer, but the fifth inning brought the same result, although Yale succeeded in getting a man to third with only one out. An attempt to sacrifice him home failed, and a double play was made, retiring the side.

Harvard opened the sixth by batting a ball straight at Yale's shortstop, who played tag with it, chasing it around his feet long enough to allow the batter to reach first. It was not a hit, but an error for short.

This seemed to break the Yale team up somewhat. The runner tried for second on the first ball pitched, and Yale's catcher overthrew, although he had plenty of time to catch the man. The runner kept on to third and got it on a slide.

Now Harvard rejoiced. Although he had not obtained a hit, the man had reached third on two errors, and there was every prospect of scoring.

Merriwell did not seem to lose his temper or his coolness. He took plenty of time to let everybody get quieted down, and then he quickly struck out the next man. The third man, however, managed to hit the ball fairly and knocked a fly into left field. It was gathered in easily, but the man on third held the bag till the fly was caught and made a desperate dash for home.

The left fielder threw well, and the ball struck in the catcher's mitt. It did not stick, however, and the catcher lost the only opportunity to stop the score.

Harvard had scored at last!

The Harvard cheer rent the air, and crimson fluttered on all sides.

Frank struck out the next man, and then Yale came to bat, resolved to do or die. But they did not do much. Yedding was as good as ever, and the fielders gathered in anything that came their way.

At the end of the eighth inning the score remained one to nothing in Harvard's favor. It looked as if Yale would receive a shut out, and that was something awful to contemplate. The "sons of Old Eli" were ready to do anything to win a score or two.

In the first half of the ninth Harvard went at it to make some more runs. One man got a hit, stole second, and went to third on an error that allowed the batter to reach first.

Sport Harris had been disappointed when Merriwell continued to remain in the box, but now he said:

"He's rattled. Here's where they kill him."

But Frank proved that he was not rattled. He tricked the man on third into getting off the bag and then threw him out in a way that brought a yell of delight from Yale men. That fixed it so the next batter could not sacrifice with the object of letting the man on third home. Then he got down to business, and Harvard was whitewashed for the last time.

"Oh, if Yale can score now!" muttered hundreds.

The first man up flied out to center, and the next man was thrown out at first. That seemed to settle it. The spectators were making preparations to leave. The Yale bat-tender, with his face long and doleful, was gathering up the sticks.

What's that? The next man got a safe hit, a single that placed him on first. Then Frank Merriwell was seen carefully selecting a bat.

"Oh, if he were a heavy hitter!" groaned many voices.

Yedding was confident—much too confident. He laughed in Frank's face. He did not think it necessary to watch the man on first closely, and so that man found an opportunity to steal second.

Two strikes and two balls had been called. Then Yedding sent in a swift one to cut the inside corner. Merriwell swung at it.

Crack! Bat and ball met fairly, and away sailed the sphere over the head of the shortstop.

"Run!"

That word was a roar. No need to tell Frank to run. In a moment he was scudding down to first, while the left fielder was going back for the ball which had passed beyond his reach. Frank kept on for second. There was so much noise he could not hear the coachers, but he saw the fielder had not secured the ball. He made third, and the excited coacher sent him home with a furious gesture.

Every man, woman and child was standing. It seemed as if every one was shouting and waving flags, hats, or handkerchiefs. It was a moment of such thrilling, nerve-tingling excitement as is seldom experienced. If Merriwell reached home Yale won; if he failed, the score was tied, for the man in advance had scored.

The fielder had secured the ball, he drove it to the shortstop, and shortstop whirled and sent it whistling home. The catcher was ready to stop Merriwell.

"Slide!"

That word Frank heard above all the commotion. He did slide. Forward he scooted in a cloud of dust. The catcher got the ball and put it onto Frank.an instant too late!

A sudden silence.

"Safe home!" rang the voice of the umpire.

Then another roar, louder, wilder, full of unbounded joy! The Yale cheer! The band drowned by all the uproar! The sight of sturdy lads in blue, delirious with delight, hugging a dust-covered youth, lifting him to their shoulders, and bearing him away in triumph. Merriwell had won his own game, and his record was made. It was a glorious finish!

"Never saw anything better," declared Harry. "Frank, you are a wonder!"

"He is that!" declared several others. "Old Yale can't get along without him."

BASEBALL JOE'S
WINNING THROW

LESTER CHADWICK

For a moment Tom stood there a bit embarrassed, for he saw that something unusual had happened.

"I—I hope I'm not intruding," he stammered. "I didn't think—I came right in as I always do. Has anything—"

"It's all right!" exclaimed Joe quickly. "We just got word that Dad has lost his patent case."

"Gee! That's too bad!" exclaimed Tom, who knew something of the affair. "What are you going to do?" "I'm going to pitch against the Resolutes, the first thing I do!" cried Joe. "After that I'll decide what's next. But is my glove mended, Clara? Come on, Tom, we mustn't be late. We're going to wallop them—just as you said."

"I hope you do!" burst out Clara.

"Play a good game and—and—don't worry," whispered Mrs. Matson to her son as he kissed her good-bye.

The team and substitutes were to go to Rocky Ford in two big stages, in time to get in some practice on the grounds that were none too familiar to them. A crowd of Silver Star "rooters" were to follow on the trolley. The captain and managers of the rival teams watched their opponents practice with sharp eyes.

"They're snappier than when they beat us before," was Darrell's conclusion.

"They've got a heap sight better pitcher in Joe than Sam Morton ever was," concluded Captain Hen Littell of the Resolutes, who twirled for his team. "I shouldn't wonder but what we'd have a mighty close game."

The last practice was over. The scattered balls had been collected, the batting list made out and final details arranged. Once more came the thrilling cry of the umpire:

"Play ball!"

The Resolutes were to bat last, and Seth Potter went up to bat first for the Stars.

"Swat it," pleaded the crowd, and Seth smiled. But he fanned the air successively as well as successfully and soon went back to the bench. Then came Fred Newton's turn and he knocked a little pop fly that was easily caught before he reached first. Captain Rankin himself was up next and managed to get to first on a swift grounder that got past the shortstop. But he died on second, for the next man up fanned. No runs for the Stars.

The Resolutes were jubilant, thinking this argued well for them, but they looked a little blank when Joe retired their first two men hitless. For Joe had started off in good form. With the first ball he delivered he knew that he was master of the horsehide at least for a time.

"But oh! I hope I don't slump!" and he almost found himself praying that such a thing would not happen.

He was in an agony of fear when he heard the crack of the bat on the ball when the third man came up. The spheroid went shooting off in center field, but by a magnificent stop Percy Parnell gathered it in and the side was retired runless. Things were not so bad for the Stars.

For the next two innings neither side got a run, though there were some scattered hits. Again was there talk of a pitchers' battle, though in the strict sense of the word this was not so, as both Joe and Hen Littell were hit occasionally, and for what would have been runs only for the efficient fielding on both sides.

"See if we can't do something this inning!" pleaded Rankin when his side came up in their half of the fourth. The lads all tried hard and Joe knocked a pretty one that was muffed by the second baseman. However, he quickly picked it up and hurled it to first. Joe got there about the same time as the ball did, and to many he seemed safe, but he was called out.

"Aw, that's rotten!" cried Tom Davis.

"Let it go!" said Darrell sharply, and Tom subsided.

The Stars got another goose egg—four straightand in their half of the fourth the Resolutes got their first run. The crowd went wild and Joe found himself clenching his hands, for the run came in because he had given a man his base on balls. The runner had successively stolen second and third, and went home on a nice fly.

"I hope I'm not going to slump!" thought Joe and there was a lump in his throat. For an instant he found himself thinking of his father's troubles, and then he firmly dismissed them from his mind. "I've got to pitch!" he told himself fiercely.

"We've got him going!" chanted the Resolute "rooters." Joe shut his teeth grimly and struck out the next man. Then he nipped the runner stealing second and threw him out with lightning speed.

That somewhat silenced the jubilant cries and when Joe managed to retire one of the Resolutes' heaviest hitters without even a bunt a big crowd rose up and cheered him.

"They're only one ahead," said Rankin as his lads came in to bat. "Let's double it now."

And double it they did, the Star boys playing like mad and getting enough hits off Littell to make two runs.

"That's the way to wallop 'em!" sang someone in the visiting crowd and the song composed for the occasion was rendered with vim.

Desperately as the Resolutes tried in their half of the fifth to catch up to their rivals, they could not do it. Joe was at his best and in that half inning did not allow a hit. He had almost perfect control, and his speed was good. Only once or twice did he pitch at all wild and then it did no harm as there was no one on base.

The sixth inning saw a run chalked up for each team, making the score three to two in favor of the Stars.

"Oh, if we can only keep this up!" exclaimed Darrell, "we'll have them. Can you do it, Joe?"

"I guess so—yes, I can!" he said with conviction.

Then came the lucky seventh, in which the Stars pounded out three runs, setting the big crowd wild with joy, and casting corresponding gloom over the cohorts of the Resolutes. The Stars now had six runs and their rivals were desperate. They even adopted unfair tactics, and several decisions of the umpire were manifestly in their favor. The crowd hooted and yelled, but the young fellow who was calling strikes and balls held to his opinion, and the Resolutes closed their half of the seventh with two runs.

"Six to four in our favor," murmured the Stars' manager. "If we can only keep this lead the game is ours."

"That word 'if' is a big one for only two letters," spoke Captain Rankin grimly. "But maybe we can." Neither side scored in the eighth and then came the final trial of the Stars unless there should be a tie, which would necessitate ten innings.

Joe was to the bat in this inning, and oh! how hard he tried for a run! He knocked a two-bagger and stole third. There was one out when Bart Ferguson came up, and Bart was a heavy hitter. But somehow he did not make good this time. He managed to connect with the ball, however, and as soon as Joe heard the crack he started for home.

But there was brilliant playing on the part of the Resolutes. With a quick throw to home the shortstop nipped Joe at the plate, and then the catcher, hurling the ball to first, got the horsehide into the baseman's hands before Bart arrived. It was a pretty double play and retired the Stars with a goose egg.

Still they had a lead of two runs and they might be able to hold their rivals down. It was a critical point in the game. As Joe took his place and faced the batter he felt his heart wildly throbbing. He knew he must hold himself well in hand or he would go to pieces. The crowd of Resolute sympathizers was hooting and yelling at him. Darrell saw how things might go and ran out to the pitcher.

"Hold hard!" he whispered. "Just take it easy. Pitch a few balls to Bart and your nerve will come back. We've *got* to win."

"And we will!" exclaimed Joe. The delivery of a few balls, while the batter stepped away from the plate, showed Joe that he still had his speed and control. He was going to be wary what kind of curves he delivered.

He struck out the first man up with an ease that at first caused him wild elation, and then he calmed himself.

"There are two more," he reasoned. "I've got to get two more— two more."

He was almost in despair when he was hit for a two-bagger by the next player, and he was in a nervous perspiration about the man stealing to third. Then Darrell signaled him to play for the batter, and Joe did, getting him out with an easy fly.

Then there was a mix-up when the next man hit, and by an error of the left fielder the man on second, who had stolen to third, went home with a run, while the man who had brought him in got to the last bag.

"That's the stuff!" yelled the crowd. "Now one more to make it a tie and another to win!"

"Steady, boys! Steady!" called Darrell, as he saw his team on the verge of a breakdown. "We can beat 'em!"

There were now two out, one run was in, a man was on third and a heavy batter was up—one of the best of the Resolutes.

"Swat it, Armstrong! Swat it!" cried the crowd, and the big left fielder smiled confidently.

"Ball one!" cried the umpire, after Joe's first delivery.

There was a gasp of protest from Bart behind the plate, for the sphere had come over cleanly. Darrell signaled to the catcher to make no protest. Joe felt a wave of anger, but he endeavored to keep cool. But when the second ball was called on him he wanted to run up and thrash the umpire. The latter was grinning derisively.

"Here's a strike!" cried Joe in desperation and he was gratified when Armstrong struck at it and missed.

"Why didn't you call that a ball?" asked Bart of the umpire. The latter did not answer.

Another ball was called and then a strike. Now came the supreme moment. Two men out, a man on third waiting to rush in with the tying run, a heavy hitter at bat and three balls and two strikes called on him. No wonder Joe's hand trembled a little.

"Easy, old man!" called Darrell to him. "You can make him fan."

Joe thought rapidly. He had studied the batter and he thought that by delivering a swift in-shoot he could fool Armstrong. It was his last chance, for another ball meant that the batter would walk, and there was even a better stick-man to follow.

Joe wound up, and sent in a swift one. His heart was fluttering, he could hardly see, there was a roaring in his ears. And then he dimly saw

Armstrong strike at the ball desperately. Almost at the same moment Joe knew he would miss it.

The ball landed in the center of Bart's big glove with a resounding whack. He held it exactly where he had caught it. Joe had delivered the winning throw.

"Strike three—batter's out!" howled the umpire, and then his voice was drowned in a yell of joy from the sympathizers of the Stars.

For their team had won! The Resolutes were retired with but one run in the ninth and the final score was five to six in favor of our friends. They had beaten their old rivals on their own grounds and they had won the county championship!

"Great work, old man! Great!" yelled Darrell in Joe's ear. "You saved the day for us."

"Nonsense!" exclaimed Joe modestly.

"Three cheers for Baseball Joe!" yelled Tom Davis, and how those cheers did ring out.

"Three cheers for the Stars—they beat us fair and square!" called Captain Littell, and this was quite a different ending than that which had marked the previous game.

Some wanted to carry Joe around on their shoulders but he slipped away, and got off his uniform. Soon the team was on its way back to Riverside.

"You ought to be in a bigger team," Darrell told Joe. "You've got the making of a great pitcher in you."

"Well, I guess I'll have to stick around here for a while yet," replied our hero, as he thought of the fallen finances of his father. Never in all his life had he so longed for the chance to go to boarding school, and thence to college. But he knew it could not be, chiefly through the treachery of Benjamin and Holdney. Joe felt a wave of resentment against them sweep over him, and his thoughts were black and bitter.

Tom walked as far as Joe's street with him. He had a silent sympathy that spoke more than mere words could have done.

"So long," he said softly as they parted. "It was a great game, Joe, and I'm almost glad you've got to stay with the Stars."

"Well, did you win?" asked his mother, as Joe entered the house—entered it more listlessly than winning a big game would seem to warrant. "Did you beat the Resolutes, Joe?"

"Yes, we did—why, Mother, what's the matter?" cried the young pitcher, for there was a look of joy and happiness on her face, a look entirely different than when he had left her after the bad news. "Has anything—anything good happened?" he asked.

"Yes!" she exclaimed, "there has. I just had another telegram from your father. Everything is all right. He gets back his patents."

"No!" cried Joe, as if unable to believe the news. "But I tell you yes!" repeated Mrs. Matson, and there was joy in her voice. "At first your father believed that all was lost, just as he wired us. Then, most unexpectedly he tells me, they were able to obtain some evidence from outside parties which they had long tried for in vain.

"It seems that a witness for Mr. Benjamin and his side, on whom they very much depended, deserted them, and went over to your father and his lawyer, and—"

"Hurray for that witness, whoever he was!" cried Joe.

"Be quiet," begged Clara, "and let Mother tell."

"There isn't much to tell," went on Mrs. Matson. "With the unexpected evidence of this witness your father's lawyer won the case, almost at the last moment. In fact your father had given up, and was about ready to leave the court when the man sent in word that he would testify for them. That was after your father sent the telegram that came just before you went off to the game, Joe."

"Oh, I'm so glad!" cried Clara.

"Now it's your turn to be quiet and listen," admonished Joe, with a smile at his sister.

"I have just about finished," went on their mother. "The judge decided in your father's favor, and he doesn't even have to share the profits of the invention with the harvester company or with Mr. Rufus Holdney, as he at one time thought he would, for they have violated their contract. So we won't be poor, after all, children. Aren't you glad?"

"You bet!" exploded Joe, throwing his arms around his mother's neck.

"And we won't have to leave this nice house," added Clara, looking around the comfortable abode. "Then I can go to boarding school—and pitch on the school nine; can't I, Mother?" cried Joe, throwing his arms around her.

"Oh, yes; I suppose so," she answered, with half a sigh. "But I do wish you'd do something else besides play baseball."

"Something else besides baseball, Mother! Why, there's nothing to be compared to it. Hurray! I'm going to boarding school! I'm going to boarding school!" and Joe, catching Clara around the waist, waltzed her around the room. Then he caught his mother on his other arm—the arm that won the victory for the Stars that day—and her, too, he whirled about until she cried for mercy.

"Oh, but this is great!" Joe cried when he stopped for breath. "Simply great! I must go and tell Tom. Maybe he can go to boarding school with me."

And whether Tom did or not, and what were our hero's further fortunes on the diamond, will be related in the next volume, to be called: "Baseball Joe on the School Nine; or, Pitching for the Blue Banner."

There was an impromptu feast that night for the victorious Silver Stars and Joe was the hero of the occasion. He was toasted again and again, and called upon to make some remarks, which he did in great confusion. But his chums thought it the best speech they had ever heard.

"Three cheers for Baseball Joe!" called Tom Davis, and the room rang with them, while Joe tried to hide his blushes by drinking glass after glass of lemonade.

And now, for a time, we will take leave of him, crying as his chums did after the great victory on the diamond: "Hurrah for Baseball Joe!"

MR. DOOLEY
ON BASEBALL

FINLEY PETER DUNNE

"D'ye iver go to a baseball game?" asked Mr. Hennessy.

"Not now," said Mr. Dooley. "I haven't got th' intellick f'r it. Whin I was a young fellow nathin' plazed me betther thin to go out to th' ball grounds, get a good cosy seat in th' sun, take off me collar an' coat an' buy a bottle iv pop, not so much, mind ye, f'r th' refrishment, because I niver was much on pop, as to have something handy to reprove th' empire with whin he give an eeronyous decision. Not only that, me boy, but I was a fine amachure ballplayer mesilf I was first baseman iv th' Prairie Wolves whin we beat th' nine iv Injine Company Five be a scoor iv four hundherd an' eight to three hundherd an' twinty-five. It was very close. Th' game started just afther low mass on a Sundah mornin' an' was called on account iv darkness at th' end iv th' fourth inning. I knocked th' ball over th' fence into Donovan's coal yard no less thin twelve times. All this talk about this here young fellow Baker makes me smile. Whin I was his age I wudden't counf annything but home-runs. If it wasn't a home-run I'd say: 'Don't mark it down' an' go back an' have another belt at th' ball. Thim were th' days.

"We usen't to think base-ball was a science. No man was very good at it that was good at annything else. A young fellow that had a clear eye in his head an' a sthrong pair iv legs undher him an' that was onaisy in th' close atmosphere iv th' school room, an' didn't like th' profissyon iv plumbing was like as not to join a ball team. He come home in th' fall with a dimon in his shirt front an' a pair iv hands on him that looked like th' boughs iv a three that's been sthruck be lightenin' and he was th' hero in th' neighborhood till his dimon melted an' he took to drivin' a thruck. But 'tis far different nowadays. To be a ball-player a man has to have a joynt intilleck. Inside base-ball, th' paapers calls it, is so deep that it'd give brain fever to a pro-fissor iv asthronomy to thry to figure it out. Each wan iv these here mathymatical janiuses has to carry a thousand mysteeryous signals in his head an' they're changed ivry day an' sometimes in the middle iv th' game. I'm so sorry f'r th' poor fellows. In th' old days whin they were through with th' game they'd maybe sthray over to th' Dutchman's f'r a pint iv beer. Now they hurry home to their study an' spind th' avnin' poorin' over books iv allgibera an' thrigynomethry.

"How do I know? Hogan was in here last night with an article on th' 'Mysthries iv Baseball.' It's be a larned man. Here it is: Th' ord-hinary observer or lunk-head who knows nawthin' about base-ball excipt what he learned be playin' it, has no idee that th' game as played to-day is wan iv th' most inthricate sciences known to mankind. In th' first place th' player must have an absolute masthry iv th' theery iv ballistic motion. This is especially true iv th' pitcher. A most exact knowledge is mathymatics is required f'r th' position. What is vulgarly known as th' spitball on account iv th' homely way in which th' op'ra-tor procures his effects is in fact a solution iv wan iv th' most inthri-cate problems in mechanics. Th' purpose iv th' pitcher is to project th' projectyle so that at a pint between his position an' th' batsman th' tindincy to pr-ceed on its way will be countheracted be an impulse to return whence it come. Th' purpose iv th' batsman is, afther judgin' be scientific methods th' probable coorse or thrajecthry iv th' missile, to oppose it with sufficyent foorce at th' proper moment an' at th' most efficient point, first to retard its forward movement, thin to correct th' osseylations an' fin'ly to propel it in a direction approximately opposite fr'm its original progress. This, I am informed, is technically known as 'bustin' th' ball on th' nose (or bugle).' In a gr-reat number iv cases which I observed th' experiment iv th' batsman failed an' th' empire was obliged so to declare, th' ball havin' actually crossed th' plate but eluded th' (intended) blow. In other cases where no blow was attimpted or aven meditated I noted that th' empire erred an' in gin'ral I must deplore an astonishin' lack in thrained scientific observation on th' part iv this officyal. He made a number iv grievous blundhers an' I was not surprised to larn fr'm a gintleman who set next to me that he (th' empire) had spint th' arly part iv his life as a fish in the Mammoth Cave iv Kentucky. I thried me best to show me disapproval iv his unscientific an' infamous methods be hittin' him over th' head with me umbrella as he left th' grounds. At th' request iv th' iditor iv th' magazine I inthervieved Misther Bugs Mulligan th' pitcher iv th' Kangaroos afther th' game. I found th' cillybrated expert in th' rotundy iv th' Grand Palace Hotel where he was settin' with other players polishin' his finger nails. I r-read him my notes on th' game an' he expressed his approval addin' with a show at laste iv enthusyasm: 'Bo, ye have a head like a dhrum.' I requested him to sign th' foregoin' statement but he declined remarkin' that th' last time he wrote his name he sprained his wrist an' was out iv the game f'r a week.

"What'd I be doin' at th' likes iv a game like that? I'd come away with a narvous headache. No, sir, whin I take a day off, I take a day off. I'm not goin' to a base-ball game. I'm goin' to take a bag iv peanuts an' spind an afthemoon at th' chimical labrytory down at th' colledge where there's something goin' on I can undherstand."

"Oh, sure," said Mr. Hennessy, "if 'twas as mysteryous as all that how cud Tom Donahue's boy Petie lam it that was fired fr'm th' Brothers School because he cuddn't add? ... "

"Annyhow 'tis a gr-rand game, Hinnissy, whether 'tis played th' way th' pro-fissor thinks or th' way Petie lamed to play it in th' backyard an' I shuddn't wondher if it's th' way he's still playin'. Th' two grreat American spoorts are a good deal alike polyticks an' baseball. They're both played be pro-fissyonals, th' teams ar-re r-run be fellows that cuddn't throw a base-ball or stuff a ballot box to save their lives an' ar-re on'y intherested in countin' up th' gate receipts, an' here ar-re we settin' out in the sun on th' bleachin' booards, payin' our good money f'r th' spoort, hot an' uncomfortable but happy, injying ivry good play, hottin' ivry bad wan, knowin' nathin' about th' inside play an' not carin', but all jinin' in th' cry iv 'Kill th' empire.' They're both grand games."

"Speakin' iv polyticks," said Mr. Hennessy, "who d'ye think'll be ilicted?"

"Afther lookin' th' candydates over," said Mr. Dooley, "an' studyin' their qualifications carefully I can't thruthfully say that I see a prisidintial possibility in sight."

JINXES AND WHAT THEY MEAN TO A BALL-PLAYER

CHRISTY MATHEWSON

A friend of mine, who took a different fork in the road when we left college from the one that I have followed, was walking down Broadway in New York with me one morning after I had joined the Giants, and we passed a cross-eyed man. I grabbed off my hat and spat in it. It was a new hat, too. "What's the matter with you, Matty?" he asked, surprised.

"Spit in your hat quick and kill that jinx," I answered, not thinking for the minute, and he followed my example.

I forgot to mention, when I said he took another fork in the road, that he had become a pitcher, too, but of a different kind. He had turned out to be sort of a conversational pitcher, for he was a minister, and, as luck would have it, on the morning we met that cross-eyed man he was wearing a silk hat. I was shocked, pained, and mortified when I saw what I had made him do. But he was the right sort, and wanted to go through with the thing according to the standards of the professional man with whom he happened to be at the time.

"What's the idea?" he asked as he replaced his hat. "Worst jinx in the world to see a cross-eyed man,"

I replied. "But I hope I didn't hurt your silk hat," I quickly apologized.

"Not at all. But how about these ball-players who masticate the weed? Do they kill jinxes, too?" he wanted to know. And I had to admit that they were the main exterminators of the jinx.

"Then," he went on, "I'm glad that the percentage of wearers of cross eyes is small."

I have just looked into one of my favorite works for that word "jinx," and found it not. My search was in Webster's dictionary. But any ball-player can give a definition of it with his hands tied behind him—that is, any one except "Arlie" Latham, and, with his hands bound, he is deaf and dumb. A jinx is something which brings bad luck to a ball-player, and the members of the profession have built up a series of lucky and unlucky omens that should be catalogued. And besides the common or garden variety of jinxes, many stars have a series of private or pet and trained ones that are more malignant in their forms than those which come out in the open. A jinx is the child of superstition, and ball-players are among the most superstitious persons in the world, notwithstanding all this conversation lately about educated men breaking into the game and paying no attention whatever to the good and bad omens. College men are coming into both the leagues, more of them each year, and they are doing their share to make the game better and the class of men higher, but they fall the hardest for the jinxes.

And I don't know as it is anything to be ashamed of at that.

A really true, on-the-level, honest-to-jiminy jinx can do all sorts of mean things to a professional ballplayer. I have seen it make a bad pitcher out of a good one, and a blind batter out of a three-hundred hitter, and I have seen it make a ball club, composed of educated men, carry a Kansas farmer, with two or three screws rattling loose in his dome, around the circuit because he came as a prophet and said that he was accompanied by Miss Fickle Fortune. And that is almost a jinx record.

Jinx and Miss Fickle Fortune never go around together. And ball-players are always trying to kill this jinx, for, once he joins the club, all hope is gone. He dies hard, and many a good hat has been ruined in an effort to destroy him, as I have said before, because the wearer happened to be chewing tobacco when the jinx dropped around. But what's a new hat against a losing streak or a batting slump?

Luck is a combination of confidence and getting the breaks. Ball-players get no breaks without confidence in themselves, and lucky omens inspire this confidence. On the other hand, unlucky signs take it away. The lucky man is the one who hits the nail on the head and not his fingers, and the ability to swat the nail on its receptive end is a combination of self-confidence and an aptitude for hammering. Good ball-playing is the combination of self-confidence and the ability to play.

The next is "Red" Ames, although designated as "Leon" by his family when a very small boy before he began to play ball. (He is still called "Leon" in the winter.) Ames is of Warren, Ohio, and the Giants, and he is said to hold the Marathon record for being the most unlucky pitcher that ever lived, and I agree with the sayers. For several seasons, Ames couldn't seem to win a ball game, no matter how well he pitched. In 1909, "Red" twirled a game on the opening day of the season against Brooklyn that was the work of a master. For nine innings he held his opponents hitless, only to have them win in the thirteenth. Time and again Ames has pitched brilliantly, to be finally beaten by a small score, because one of the men behind him made an error at a critical moment, or because the team could not give him any runs by which to win. No wonder the newspapers began to speak of Ames as the "hoodoo" pitcher and the man "who couldn't win."

There was a cross-eyed fellow who lived between Ames and the Polo Grounds, and "Red" used to make a detour of several blocks en route to the park to be sure to miss him in case he should be out walking. But one day in 1911, when it was his turn to pitch, he bumped into that cross-eyed man and, in spite of the fact that he did his duty by his hat and got three or four small boys to help him out, he failed to last two innings. When it came time to go West on the final trip of the 1911 season, Ames was badly discouraged.

"I don't see any use in taking me along, Mac," he said to McGraw a few days before we left. "The club can't win with me pitching if the other guys don't even get a foul."

The first stop was in Boston, and on the day we arrived it rained. In the mail that day, addressed to Leon Ames, came a necktie and a four-leaf clover from a prominent actress, wishing Ames good luck. The directions were inside the envelope. The fourleaf clover, if the charm were to work, must be worn on both the uniform and street clothes, and the necktie was to be worn with the street clothes and concealed in the uniform, if that necktie could be concealed anywhere. It would have done for a headlight and made Joseph's coat of many colors look like a mourning garment.

"Might as well wish good luck to a guy on the way to the morgue," murmured Ames as he surveyed the layout, but he manfully put on the necktie, taking his first dose of the prescription, as directed, at once, and he tucked the four-leaf clover away carefully in his wallet.

"You've got your work cut out for you, old boy," he remarked to the charm as he put it away, "but I'd wear you if you were a horseshoe."

The first day that Ames pitched in Boston he won, and won in a stroll.

"The necktie," he explained that night at dinner, and pointed to the three-sheet, colored-supplement affair he was wearing around his collar, "I don't change her until I lose."

And he didn't lose a game on that trip. Once he almost did, when he was taken out in the sixth inning, and a batter put in for him, but the Giants finally pulled out the victory and he got the credit for it. He swept through the West unbeatable, letting down Pittsburg with two or three hits, cleaning up in St. Louis, and finally breaking our losing streak in Chicago after two games had gone against us. And all the time he wore that spectrum around his collar for a necktie. As it frayed with the wear and tear, more colors began to show, although I didn't think it possible. If he had had occasion to put on his evening clothes, I believe that tie would have gone with it.

For my part, I would almost rather have lost a game and changed the necktie, since it gave one the feeling all the time that he was carrying it around with him because he had had the wrong end of an election bet, or something of the sort. But not Ames! He was a game guy. He stuck with the necktie, and it stuck with him, and the combination kept right on winning ball games. Maybe he didn't mind it because he could not see it himself, unless he looked in a mirror, but it was rough on the rest of the team, except that we needed the games the necktie won, to take the pennant.

Columns were printed in the newspapers about that necktie, and it became the most famous scarf in the world. Ames used to sleep with it under his pillow alongside of his bank roll, and he didn't lose another game until the very end of the season, when he dropped one against Brooklyn.

"I don't hardly lay that up against the tie," he said afterwards. "You see, Mac put all those youngsters into it, and I didn't get any support."

Analyzing is a distasteful pastime to me, but let's see what it was that made Ames win. Was it the necktie? Perhaps not. But some sliver of confidence, which resulted from that first game when he was dressed up in the scarf and the four-leaf clover, got stuck in his mind. And after that the rest was easy.

Frank Chance, the manager of the Cubs, has a funny superstition which is of the personal sort. Most ball-players have a natural prejudice against the number "13" in any form, but particularly when attached to a Pullman berth. But Chance always insists, whenever possible, that he have "lower 13." He says that if he can just crawl in under that number he is sure of a good night's rest, a safe journey, and a victory the next day. He has been in two or three minor railroad accidents, and he declares that all these occurred when he was sleeping on some other shelf besides "lower 13." He can usually satisfy his hobby, too, for most travellers steer clear of the berth.

McGraw believes a stateroom brings him good luck, or at least he always insists on having one when he can get it.

"Chance can have 'lower 13,'" says "Mac," "but give me a stateroom for luck."

Most ball-players nowadays treat the superstitions of the game as jokes, probably because they are a little ashamed to acknowledge their weaknesses, but away down underneath they observe the proprieties of the ritual. Why, even I won't warm up with the third baseman while I am waiting for the catcher to get on his mask and the rest of his paraphernalia. Once, when I first broke in with the Giants, I warmed up with the third baseman between innings and in the next round they hit me hard and knocked me out of the box. Since then I have had an uncommon prejudice against the practice, and I hate to hear a man even mention it. Devlin knows of my weakness and never suggests it when he is playing the bag, but occasionally a new performer will drill into the box score at third base and yell:

"Come on, Matty! Warm up here while you're waiting."

It gets me. I'll pitch to the first baseman or a substitute catcher to keep warm, but I would rather freeze to death than heat up with the third baseman. That is one of my pet jinxes.

And speaking of Arthur Devlin, he has a few hand-raised jinxes of his own, too. For instance, he never likes to hear a player hum a tune on the bench, because he thinks it will keep him from getting a base hit. He nearly beat a youngster to death one day when he kept on humming after Devlin had told him to stop.

"Cut that out, Caruso," yelled Arthur, as the recruit started his melody. "You are killing base hits."

The busher continued with his air until Devlin tried another form of persuasion.

Arthur also has a favorite seat on the bench which he believes is luckier than the rest, and he insists on sitting in just that one place.

But the worst blow Devlin ever had was when some young lady admirer of his in his palmy days, who unfortunately wore her eyes crossed, insisted on sitting behind third base for each game, so as to be near him. Arthur noticed her one day and, after that, it was all off. He hit the worst slump of his career. For a while no one could understand it, but at last he confessed to McGraw.

"Mac," he said one night in the club-house, "it's that jinx. Have you noticed her? She sits behind the bag every day, and she has got me going. She has sure slid the casters under me. I wish we could bar her out, or poison her, or shoot her, or chloroform her, or kill her in some nice, mild way because, if it isn't done, this League is going to lose a ball-player. How can you expect a guy to play with that overlooking him every afternoon?"

McGraw took Devlin out of the game for a time after that, and the newspapers printed several yards about the cross-eyed jinx who had ruined the Giants' third baseman.

With the infield weakened by the loss of Devlin, the club began to lose with great regularity. But one day the jinxess was missing and she never came back. She must have read in the newspapers what she was doing to Devlin, her hero, and quit the national pastime or moved to another part of the stand. With this weight off his shoulders, Arthur went back into the game and played like mad.

"If she'd stuck much longer," declared McGraw, joyous in his rejuvenated third baseman, "I would have had her eyes operated on and straightened. This club couldn't afford to keep on losing ball games because you are such a Romeo, Arthur, that even the cross-eyed ones fall for you."

Ball-players are very superstitious about the bats. Did you ever notice how the clubs are all laid out in a neat, even row before the bench and are scrupulously kept that way by the bat boy? If one of the sticks by any chance gets crossed, all the players will shout:

"Uncross the bats! Uncross the bats!"

It's as bad as discovering a three-alarm fire in an excelsior factory. Don't believe it? Then listen to what happened to the Giants once because a careless bat boy neglected his duty. The team was playing in Cincinnati in the season of 1906 when one of the bats got crossed through the carelessness of the boy. What was the result? "Mike" Donlin, the star slugger of the team, slid into third base and came up with a broken ankle.

Ever since that time we have carried our own boy with us, because a club with championship aspirations cannot afford to take a chance with those foreign artists handling the bats. They are likely to throw you down at any time.

The Athletics have a funny superstition which is private or confined to their team as far as I know. When luck seems to be breaking against them in a game, they will take the bats and throw them wildly into the air and let them lie around in front of their bench, topsy-turvy. They call this changing the luck, but any other club would consider that it was the worst kind of a jinx. It is the same theory that cardplayers have about shuffling the deck vigorously to bring a different run of fortune. Then, if the luck changes, the Athletics throw the bats around some more to keep it. This act nearly cost them one of their best ball-players in the third game of the 1911 world's series.

The Philadelphia players had tossed their bats to break their run of luck, for the score was 1 to 0 against them, when Baker came up in the ninth inning. He cracked his now famous home run into the right-field bleachers, and the men on the bench hurled the bats wildly into the air. In jumping up and reaching for a bat to throw, Jack Barry, the shortstop, hit his head on the concrete roof of the structure and was stunned for a minute. He said that little black specks were floating in front of his eyes, but he gamely insisted on playing the contest out. "Connie" Mack was so worried over his condition that he sent Ira Thomas out on the field to inquire if he were all right, and this interrupted the game in the ninth inning. A lot of the spectators thought that Thomas was out there, bearing some secret message from "Connie" Mack. None knew that he was ascertaining the health of a player who had almost killed himself while killing a jinx.

The Athletics, for two seasons, have carried with them on all their trips a combination bat boy and mascot who is a hunchback, and he out jinxed our champion jinx killer, Charley Faust, in the 1911 world's series. A hunchback is regarded by ballplayers as the best luck in the world. If a man can just touch that hump on the way to the plate, he is sure to get a hit, and any observant spectator will notice the Athletics' hitters rubbing the hunchback boy before leaving the bench. So attached to this boy have the players become that they voted him half a share of the prize money last year after the world's series. Lots of ball-players would tell you that he deserved it because he has won two world's pennants for them.

Another great piece of luck is for a ball-player to rub a colored kid's head. I've walked along the street with ball-players and seen them stop a young negro and take off his hat and run their hands through his kinky hair. Then I've seen the same ball-player go out and get two or three hits that afternoon and play the game of his life. Again, it is the confidence inspired, coupled with the ability.

Another old superstition among ball-players is that a load of empty barrels means base hits. If an athlete can just pass a flock of them on the way to the park, he is sure to step right along stride for stride with the three-hundred hitters that afternoon. McGraw once broke up a batting slump of the Giants with a load of empty barrels. That is why I maintain he is the greatest manager of them all. He takes advantage of the little things, even the superstitions of his men, and turns them to his account. He played this trick in one of the first years that he managed the New York club. The batting of all the players had slumped at the same time. None could hit, and the club was losing game after game as a result, because the easiest pitchers were making the best batters look foolish. One day Bowerman came into the clubhouse with a smile on his face for the first time in a week.

"Saw a big load of empty barrels this afternoon, boys," he announced, "and just watch me pickle the pill out there to-day."

Right at that point McGraw got an idea, as he frequently does. Bowerman went out that afternoon and made four hits out of a possible five. The next day three or four more of the players came into the park, carrying smiles and the announcement that fortunately they, too, had met a load of empty barrels. They, then, all went out and regained their old batting strides, and we won that afternoon for the first time in a week. More saw a load of barrels the next day and started to bat. At last all the members of the team had met the barrels, and men with averages of .119 were threatening to chisel into the three-hundred set. With remarkable regularity the players were meeting loads of empty barrels on their way to the park, and, with remarkable regularity and a great deal of expedition, the pitchers of opposing clubs were being driven to the shower bath.

"Say," asked "Billy" Gilbert, the old second baseman, of "Bill" Lauder, formerly the protector of the third corner, one day, "is one of that team of horses sorrel and the other white?"

"Sure," answered "Bill."

"Sure," echoed McGraw. "I hired that load of empty barrels by the week to drive around and meet you fellows on the way to the park, and you don't think I can afford to have them change horses every day, do you?"

Everybody had a good laugh and kept on swatting. McGraw asked for waivers on the load of empty barrels soon afterwards, but his scheme had stopped a batting slump and put the club's hitters on their feet again. He plays to the little personal qualities and superstitions in the men to get the most out of them. And just seeing those barrels gave them the idea that they were bound to get the base hits, and they got them. Once more, the old confidence, hitched up with ability.

What manager would have carried a Kansas farmer around the circuit with him besides McGraw? I refer to Charles Victor Faust of Marion, Kansas, the most famous jinx killer of them all. Faust first met the Giants in St. Louis on the next to the last trip the club made West in the season of 1911, when he wandered into the Planter's Hotel one day, asked for McGraw and announced that a fortune teller of Marion had informed him he would be a great pitcher and that for $5 he could have a full reading. This pitching announcement piqued Charles, and he reached down into his jeans, dug out his last five, and passed it over. The fortune teller informed Faust that all he had to do to get into the headlines of the newspapers and to be a great pitcher was to join the New York Giants. He joined, and, after he once joined, it would have taken the McNamaras in their best form to separate him from the said Giants.

"Charley" came out to the ball park and amused himself warming up. Incidentally, the Giants did not lose a game while he was in the neighborhood. The night the club left for Chicago on that trip, he was down at the Union Station ready to go along.

"Did you get your contract and transportation?" asked McGraw, as the lanky Kansan appeared.

"No," answered "Charley."

"Pshaw," replied McGraw. "I left it for you with the clerk at the hotel. The train leaves in two minutes," he continued, glancing at his watch. "If you can run the way you say you can, you can make it and be back in time to catch it."

It was the last we saw of "Charley" Faust for a time—galloping up the platform in his angular way with that contract and transportation in sight.

"I'm almost sorry we left him," remarked McGraw as "Charley" disappeared in the crowd. We played on around the circuit with indifferent luck and got back to New York with the pennant no more than a possibility, and rather a remote one at that. The first day we were in New York "Charley" Faust entered the clubhouse with several inches of dust and mud caked on him, for he had come all the way either by side-door special or blind baggage.

"I'm here, all right," he announced quietly, and started to climb into a uniform.

"I see you are," answered McGraw.

"Charley" stuck around for two or three days, and we won. Then McGraw decided he would have to be dropped and ordered the man on the door of the clubhouse to bar this Kansas kid out. Faust broke down and cried that day, and we lost. After that he became a member of the club, and we won game after game until some busy newspaper man obtained a vaudeville engagement for him at a salary of $100 a week. We lost three games the week he was absent from the grounds, and Faust saw at once he was not doing the right thing by the club, so, with a wave of his hand that would have gone with J. P. Morgan's income, he passed up some lucrative vaudeville contracts, much to the disgust of the newspaper man, who was cutting the remuneration with him, and settled down to business. The club did not lose a game after that, and it was decided to take Faust West with us on the last and famous trip in 1911. Daily he had been bothering McGraw and Mr. Brush for his contract, for he wanted to pitch. The club paid him some money from time to time to meet his personal expenses.

The Sunday night the club left for Boston, a vaudeville agent was at the Grand Central Station with a contract offering Faust $100 a week for five weeks, which "Charley" refused in order to stick with the club. It was the greatest trip away from home in the history of baseball. Starting with the pennant almost out of reach, the Giants won eighteen and lost four games. One contest that we dropped in St. Louis was when some of the newspaper correspondents on the trip kidnapped Faust and sat him on the St. Louis bench.

Another day in St. Louis the game had gone eleven innings, and the Cardinals needed one run to win. They had several incipient scores on the bases and "Rube" Marquard, in the box, was apparently going up in the air. Only one was out. Faust was warming up far in the suburbs when, under orders from McGraw, I ran out and sent him to the bench, for that was the place from which his charm seemed to be the most potent. "Charley" came loping to the bench as fast as his long legs would transport him and St. Louis didn't score and we won the game. It was as nice a piece of pinch mascoting as I ever saw. The first two games that "Charley" really lost were in Chicago. And all through the trip, he reiterated his weird prophecies that "the Giants with Manager McGraw were goin' ta win." The players believed in him, and none would have let him go if it had been necessary to support him out of their own pockets. And we did win.

"Charley," with his monologue and great good humor, kept the players in high spirits throughout the journey, and the feeling prevailed that we couldn't lose with him along. He was advertised all over the circuit, and spectators were going to the ball park to see Faust and Wagner. "Charley" admitted that he could fan out Hans because he had learned how to pitch out there in Kansas by correspondence school and had read of "Hans's" weakness in a book. His one "groove" was massages and manicures. He would go into the barber shop with any member of the team who happened to be getting shaved and take a massage and manicure for the purpose of sociability, as a man takes a drink. He easily was the record holder for the manicure Marathon, hanging up the figures of five in one day in St. Louis. He also liked pie for breakfast, dinner and supper, and a small half before retiring.

But, alas! "Charley" lost in the world's series. He couldn't make good. And a jinx killer never comes back. He is gone. And his expansive smile and bump-the-bumps slide are gone with him. That is, McGraw hopes he is gone. But he was a wonder while he had it. And he did a great deal toward giving the players confidence. With him on the bench, they thought they couldn't lose, and they couldn't. It has long been a superstition among ball-players that when a "bug" joins a club, it will win a championship, and the Giants believed it when "Charley" Faust arrived. Did "Charley" Faust win the championship for the Giants?

Another time-honored superstition among ballplayers is that no one must say to a pitcher as he goes to the box for the eighth inning:

"Come on, now. Only six more men." Or for the ninth:

"Pitch hard, now. Only three left."

Ames says that he lost a game in St. Louis once because McGraw forgot himself and urged him to pitch hard because only three remained to be put out. Those three batters raised the mischief with Ames's prospects; he was knocked out of the box in that last inning, and we lost the game. That was before the days of the wonder necktie.

Ames won the third game played in Chicago on the last trip West. Coming into the ninth inning, he had the Cubs beaten, when McGraw began:

"Come on, 'Red,' only—"

"Nix, Mac," cut in Ames, "for the love of Mike, be reasonable."

And then he won the game. But the chances are that if McGraw had got that "only three more" out, he would have lost, because it would have been working on his strained nerves.

ONE DOWN 713 TO GO

DAMON RUNYON

There is not enough of Hughy High to make one good-sized hero for our story this morning, and so we add to him Luther Cook and thus compile a sufficient subject. Hughy and Luther, bunched together, make something to talk about. They assisted this community in taking a notable decision over the municipality of Boston, Mass., yesterday afternoon.

The shades of the thirteenth inning were falling fast up at the Polo Grounds, and the Wild Yanks and the Boston Red Sox, champspresumptive of the Amur-r-r-ick-kin League, as Ban Johnson calls it, were clustered in a tie. The count was three all, with Will Evans, the gesticulator, eagerly scanning the horizon for evidence of nightfall, when Hughy and Luther amalgamated and broke up the pastime, the final tally being 4 to 3 in favor of the grand old Empire State.

In our own garrulous way we shall now endeavor to tell you just how it happened, omitting only such details as we deem unfit for publication.

Hughy High, small, but efficient, opened that thirteenth with a single to centre. Walter Pipp struck out, Hughy High stole second. Luther Cook singled over Heine Wagner's head, just out of Heine Wagner's reach and mid the mad mumble of the multitude. Hughy

High came tumbling in across the h.p. with the winning run. How was that for High?

Having described the most important incident of the game, we now feel constrained to warn the compositors to clear away all obstructions below, and to either side, so we can run right on down this column, and over into the next, in telling about the goings-on prior to the moment mentioned, beginning with that hour in the ninth when we boys tied 'er up.

Luther Cook figured in that, too. One was out in the ninth, when George Ruth struck Luther with a pitched baseball. George pitched the baseball lefthanded, and by giving it the body-follow-through, he succeeded in raising a tumor on Luther's shoulder. Cap'n Roger Peckinpaugh subsided without a struggle, while Luther tarried at first, rubbing his wounded torso, and glaring at George Ruth. That made two out, and it looked as this story would have to open with sighs, when Luther Boone—but by all means a separate paragraph for Luther.

Luther Boone doubled to right, a solid, smacking, soulful double that knocked the bleacherites back on the butt of their spines from the crouch that precedes the rush for the exits, and which scored Luther Cook with the tying tally.

A moment later Luther Boone went on to third, when George Ruth made a bad throw trying to catch him off second, but Leslie Nunamaker could not bring him in, and the game passed on into extra innings and to the big punch in the story as outlined above.

Well, it was quite a pastime. Everybody said it was a great game to win. Everybody was so delighted that they almost forgot about Dominick Mullaney, who was cast for the character of the bad guy in this tale. Not that we intend to make Dominick out, because you know the size of Dominick. The day that we blacken the character of Dominick is the day after Dominick leaves town, and gets well beyond the confines of this newspaper's circulation.

In the seventh inning, with we 'uns needing a run to tie, Luther Cook singled. Peckinpaugh was duly expunged, and Boone hit the right field wall with a blow which put cook [sic] on third. The ball hopped back off the razor-backed sign in [sic] right into Hooper's hands, and Hooper threw to first, instead of second, as Boone anticipated.

Boone had taken "that old turn" after hitting first, in accordance with the advice of all the coaches, and was several feet off the bag when Hoblitzel got the ball. Dominick said he was out, and the rally bogged down right there.

The crowd discussed Dominick in audible tones on account of that decision, and some thought it might be a good thing to assassinate him at once, but no action was taken on account of Dominick's size, and the presence of Ban Johnson.

We have been wondering ever since the season opened why Wild Bill Donovan has been keeping little Jack Warhop warmed up down there in right field, and the reason developed yesterday. It was for the purpose of having Jack pitch this game, and Jack pitched very well indeed while he was pitching, proving the efficacy of warming-up.

In the eighth inning, Charles Mullen batted for Jack, but nothing came of it, as Mike McNally, the Sox's new third baser, and the noisiest man in the whole world, next to Baumgartner, the Phil pitcher, made a smashing play on Charley's drive. Fritz Maisel got an infield hit that inning, stole second, moved to third on Carrigan's bad throw, and scored on Hartzell's out.

Cyrus Pieh finished the game for the Yanks, and this story would be wholly incomplete without an eulogy of Cyrus. Tall, thin and very interesting, Cyrus would have a column all to himself did space permit.

He compiled a masterly finish. Pieh had the crust, as you might say, to use a slow curve on some of the sluggers of the Sox, and he made them appear mighty futile and inefficient.

In the eleventh he gathered up Scott's slow roller and made a two-base bad chuck to Pipp. Then he fanned McNally. Henricksen, who once broke up a world's series pastime on Chris Mathewson—long and long ago, that seems—batted for Cyrus Pieh any time he feels that way about it.

Henricksen singled and Scott took third, Henricksen moving to second on the throw in. Then Cyrus Pieh fanned Ruth and Hooper. How was that for Peih?

Fanning this Ruth is not as easy as the name and occupation might indicate. In the third frame Ruth knocked the slant out of one of Jack Warhop's underhanded subterfuges, and put the baseball in the right field stand for a home run.

Ruth was discovered by Jack Dunn in a Baltimore school a year ago when he had not yet attained his lefthanded majority, and was adopted, and adapted, by Jack for the uses of the Orioles. He is now quite a pitcher and a demon hitter—when he connects.

In our boys' end of the eleventh, Pipp led off with a single, but Wild Bill had Cook up there trying to sacrifice, and after failing in two attempts to bunt, Cook struck out. Whereupon he flung his bat far from him and took on an expression of intense disgust. Evidently the only way Luther likes to bunt is from his shoe cleats.

It was in that inning that Luther Boone was purposely passed for the first time in his brief career. In other days pitchers would have passed the whole batting order to get at Luther, but yesterday Ruth let him go to fire at Nunamaker, and Leslie did not betray Ruth's confidence. He lifted a fly to Hooper.

HOW I LOST THE 1915 WORLD SERIES

GROVER CLEVELAND ALEXANDER

The World Series was a disappointment to me. It was not so much the result, which went against my team, Philadelphia, but my own individual showing, which was so far from what I hoped it might be. Everyone knows by now that the Boston Red Sox beat us with four victories to our one, but I feel it might have been considerably different if I had lived up to expectation.

I have never yet given alibis and I am not going to begin now. But I would like to explain to my fans and friends why I think I failed in the series.

Let me begin with a day during the last month of the pennant race. It was Labor Day. We opened a crucial series with Brooklyn. The club was right on our heels and our manager Pat Moran and his boys felt, with good reason, that we must come out on the winning side of this encounter. I believe no one on our team even considered that we might not win a single contest. That is, of course, exactly what happened.

I was picked to pitch the opener. Moran depended a great deal upon winning that game. If we won, we'd have that one on ice and we'd be confident besides. It is my own feeling that Moran did not exaggerate the importance of winning that first game. I always feel that a visiting team should put its best foot forward. The home team has obvious advantages, and it is important for a visiting manager to balance those advantages as soon as he possibly can.

Larry Cheney was on the mound for the Brooks. He was lately acquired from the Cubs, and I detected an unusual determination on his part to justify the move that had brought him from Chicago.

Brooklyn scored one run off me in the first inning. After that the game settled down into one of those contests where neither team will budge an inch and the pitcher must work his heart out. Cheney, while wild, as is natural with spitball pitchers, was invincible. We could not make a single hit off him for six innings. In the seventh, he strained himself and was obliged to leave the box. It was then that our boys fell on the opposition and drove in three runs.

We began the eighth with a two-run lead. Moran felt that the game was won. I hoped it was myself when Jake Daubert went out on the first ball pitched. But then something happened. I have never been able to understand it, but in some way I strained my shoulder and the muscles in my back. I have the misfortune of getting a blister on my middle finger from throwing the ball. I remember I had a blister on that finger Labor Day, and it bothered me considerably. The ball player doesn't pay much attention to minor injuries, but try as he will a twirler can hardly get normal results from his pitching hand when his fingers are sore. I know that I unconsciously tried to humor that blistered finger. In doing so I brought the muscles of my shoulder into play in an unusual manner. Pitching a fast ball to the next man up, I strained my shoulder. I immediately felt it, and I couldn't seem to control the ball so well. When I put forth all my strength and tried to get the ball over the plate it would go outside. When I cut down a little on the stuff I was serving up, the Brooklyn batters would hit me.

I remember that I overheard a loud-voiced rooter in the stand when that inning began. The Brooklyn crowd seemed discouraged when we piled up those three runs. This particular rooter yelled out: "Never mind, boys. Go at Alexander. He's human like the rest of us."

He was certainly right. I felt human enough when they started to pound me around the lot. And I felt extremely human when at the end of that inning they had scored five runs off my delivery and snatched away a game that I had considered as good as won.

It was a bitter blow to Moran—and that Brooklyn series never got any better. We lost all three games. The third defeat ended in an accident to our first-string catcher, Reindeer Bill Killefer. My own thoughts as to the prospects for the pennant were gloomy. I worked my best with Killefer. He understood me and knew how to handle my peculiarities. However, on that score my pessimism was unnecessary. Ed Burns, Killefer's replacement, did a fine job through the closing laps of the pennant race.

I didn't tell Moran that I wrenched my shoulder during the Labor Day game. I knew he had enough on his mind without thinking about me. I was lucky enough to pitch a one-hit game against the Braves that clinched the pennant. That gave me, momentarily, the feeling that the shoulder might not disrupt me through the most important games of my career—the World Series.

It has never been my disposition to worry about things, but if there was one time in my whole life when I wanted to be in best pitching form it was for those World Series games. I would willingly have given my share of the receipts to have been able to pitch my team to a championship of the world. That is my answer to the oft-repeated suggestion that we ball players think only of the money that there is in the game.

The papers, unconsciously no doubt, added to the burden of my position. Many pitchers can work in great form when nothing in particular is at stake but crumple badly in a pinch. I do not believe I have ever faltered when I was asked to carry a heavy load, but it is human nature to feel responsibilities and to be weighted down by them. The papers spoke of Christy Mathewson and what he did in the famous series of 1905 (Matty pitched three shutouts). They said he won the series singlehanded. Some of my friends were good enough to predict equal success for me.

It is a fine thing to have friends who are confident in you, but I may say the responsibility of pitching in the World Series is enough in itself without the added consideration of living up to high expectations.

They said I was nervous in the first game. All right, I was. They hit me pretty hard, but that didn't worry me. There was a time when I used to burn up all my stuff on every ball pitched, but the pitcher grows wiser as he grows older. The fact that Boston was hitting me didn't worry me as long as I was able to keep the hits well scattered. What worried me most was the fact that our boys didn't seem to be able to hit Ernie Shore as much as the Red Sox were hitting me. At that, they only put their hits together in a single inning. They scored one run. However, I must admit in fairness that Shore had very hard luck and the breaks went badly against him. We won, 3–1.

The pitcher knows when he is not right. It is a miserable experience to know you are not at your best when you are facing a pennant winner and the world's championship is at stake.

That thought came to me with overwhelming force in the first contest, and I had to fight against it all through the series. Perhaps I allowed too much for it. As I look back upon the series now, I can criticize myself because at times I was too careful, too exact, too conscious of myself. When I am at my best I can get the ball to break as I want it to, instinctively; with little effort. And I can get my fast ball to sweep across the plate just where I tell it to go. The pitcher can always work best when he has to use the least thought and care. The more he tries to supplement tired muscles or aching joints by mental effort, the more he loses the edge he may have had on the opposition. I tried to foresee every contingency, to guard against every accident, because I was not right. Had I been in my best form, I would have given those things scarcely a second thought. I would have pitched the best I could and trusted the ability of my fielders.

Again, the pitcher in a World Series game has none of the assurance that he may have during the season. In the short series he has to do whatever he is going to do then or never at all. If a slip occurs it is too late to change it. He has one or two, or at the most three chances to deliver, and if he fails it is too late. During the season if he loses a game or two successive games it doesn't matter so much. He feels that he will have time later on to redeem himself and comforts himself with the thought that the best of them can't win all the time.

In my second game, and the game that was destined to be my last, I had hoped I might feel in perfect shape. It was the third game of the series. Boston had taken the second game 2–1.

We got off to an early lead with a run in the third, but Boston came back with a score in the fourth. From the fourth until the ninth Dutch Leonard and I were knotted in a pitcher's duel. I think I was pitching better than I did in the first game, but as fate would have it Leonard was pitching even better. The crucial point for me came in the last of the ninth. With the potential winning run on base I elected to pitch to Duffy Lewis. My critics contend that I should have elected to pass Lewis, a .291 hitter in the regular season, and pitched instead to Larry Gardner, who had a season's mark in the neighborhood of .250. That thought occurred to me, too, but I decided to pitch to Lewis for several reasons. In the first place, he had been going great guns in the series, and I figured the percentages were bound to catch up with him.

Besides, I had faced him in twelve games in a previous All-Star tour, and he had made only two hits off me. On one occasion I had struck him out four straight times. Furthermore, I estimated Gardner as a far more dangerous man in a pinch.

All my reasons notwithstanding, I was wrong. It was Lewis' hit that won the game. However, had I passed Lewis and Gardner hit me safely, I'm sure these same critics would have leveled the same complaint. The ball player becomes accustomed to the second guess, in which the press writer seems to find a delight.

I have no desire to take anything away from the reputation of Duffy Lewis. He had a wonderful series. But regardless of the results, I still feel that I was right in pitching to him. It may have been the most disastrous decision of my career, but even in defeat my reason compels me to stick by it.

After my loss in the third game, I know our team felt down and out. That depression may very well have made the difference in the score of the fourth game, which Boston won, 2–1. It was Ernie Shore who won that one for Boston. It is an interesting note that he gave us seven hits in this game, which he won, compared to the five hits he gave us in the first game, which he lost.

Behind three games to one, our hopes were all but shattered. A great deal has been written about the fifth game. I was slated to pitch and, in fact, intended to pitch up till the last moment. I never wanted to pitch a game so much in my life. How I would have loved to beat Boston in that fifth game and put us back in the series!

But I knew when I started to warm up that I wasn't right. Once again I had to make a decision. I had to choose between my own instinctive desire to pitch and my knowledge that I was in no condition to properly represent my team. I decided to tell Moran how I felt.

I must give him credit for taking this information without any great demonstration of disappointment.

"If you are not right, Alex," he said, "the rest of us will have to carry it."

Moran expressed a fine sentiment, but unfortunately it didn't work out so well. It was Mr. Lewis again who was our nemesis. He belted a lusty home run into the bleachers and Harry Hooper put the game on ice with his second home run of the contest. Again, it was a game decided in the ninth inning and Boston won, 5–4.

I do not wish to disparage the work of our pitchers, Jim Mayer and Jeptha Rixey. They did a fine job. Had the fates of the game been kinder in the ninth, they would have gained a deserved victory. But be that as it may, as long as I live I will always wonder how I might have fared had I pitched that fatal fifth game of the '15 series.

I shall always think of this series as a great personal disappointment. I was unable to live up to the expectations of my friends, and I didn't come through for my team. No matter what anyone else may say, I know the reason I lost the 1915 World Series was that I was not in the proper physical condition to give it my best.

THE CRAB

GERALD BEAUMONT

Not until the orchestra at 11:30, with a cheery flourish from the clarinets, launched into a quaint little melody, did the Crab's expression of disapproval change. Then his eyes sought a velvet curtain stretched across one end of the room. The drapery parted to admit a slip of a girl in a pink dress who came gliding down between the tables, slim white arms swaying in rhythm with her song. The Crab, obeying a sentiment he did not try to analyze, eyed her just as he had done every night for a week.

Those at the tables who had been there before nudged newcomers and whispered, "Watch her smile—it's the whole show."

It was a bright little tune—soothing as a lullaby. She sang the second chorus, looking straight at the Crab:

"Smile a-while, and I'll smile, too, What's the good of feeling blue?
Watch my lips—I'll show you how:
That's the way—you're smiling now!"

A spotlight from the balcony darted across the room and encompassed the girl and the man to whom she was singing. Amid general laughter and applause, the Crab squirmed, reddened and achieved a sheepish grin.

The singer passed to other tables, the light playing on her yellow hair and accentuating the slimness of her figure.

"I'm the Smile Girl, so folks say—
Seems like smiles all come my way.
Want to smile? I'll show you how:
That's the way—you're smiling now."

People continued smiling and humming to the tuneful melody long after she had declined further encores. The Crab stared into the bottom of his empty glass. His face was still very red. Her fingers had brushed the Crab's sleeve as lightly as a butterfly's wing but he was exalted by the contact.

Coast League fans said of Bill Crowley that if he ever learned to moderate his crabbing, the majors would one day be bidding for the greatest third baseman in history. He was chain lightning on his feet and could hit around .290 in any company. Moreover, he had perfect baseball hands, an arm of steel, and the runner was yet to wear spikes who could scare him into exposing even a corner of the bag if the play was close.

But Bill was a crab by instinct, preference and past performances. He was hard-boiled in the dye of discontent, steeped in irritability—a consistent, chronic, quarrelsome crab, operating apparently with malice aforethought and intent to commit mischief.

Naturally the fans rode him. It is human nature to poke sticks at a crab and turn it over on its back. In time, a crustacean becomes imbued with the idea that it was born to be tormented, hence it moves around with its claws alert for pointed sticks. That was the way with Bill Crowley, third-sacker extraordinary, and kicker plenipotentiary to the court of Brick McGovern, sorrel-topped manager of the Wolves. Looking for trouble, he found it everywhere.

At that, Bill the Crab was not without a certain justification. A third baseman has enough woes without being afflicted with boils on the back of his neck. Such ailments belong by the law of retribution to the outfield. The fact that little pink protuberances appeared every now and then due south from the Crab's collar button, where the afternoon sun could conveniently find them, was further proof that even Providence had joined in the general persecution.

No infielder or outfielder ever threw the ball right to the Crab. It was either too low, or too high, or too late, or on his "meat" hand. There wasn't a scorer on the circuit who knew the definition of a base hit. The only time the umpires were ever on top of the play was when Bill was the runner, and then they had their thumbs in the air before he even hit the dirt.

Under such circumstances there was nothing for the Crab to do but register his emphatic disapproval. This he invariably accomplished by slamming his glove on the ground and advancing on the umpire stiff-legged after the manner of a terrier approaching a strange dog. Had there been hair on the back of his neck, it would have bristled.

The arbiters of the diamond took no chances with the Crab. They waved five fingers at him when he took the first step, and held up both hands when he took the second. If that didn't hold him, they promptly bestowed the Order of the Tin Can by waving the right arm in the general direction of the shower baths. This meant in all a fine of twenty dollars and the familiar line in the sporting extras:

Crowley Thrown Out For Crabbing

In the last game of the season, the Crab distinguished himself by clouting a home run in the first inning with the bases full, but before the contest was over he was led from the park by two policemen, having planted his cleats on the sensitive toes of Umpire Bull Feeney and thereby precipitated the worst riot of the year.

McGovern, astute pilot of a club which had won two pennants, clung to the Crab in the forlorn hope that time and patience might work one of those miracles of the diamond which are within the memory of most veteran managers.

Had any one told the red-headed campaigner that he would yet live to see the day when the Crab would be a spineless thing of milk and water, pulling away from a runner's spikes, flinching under the taunts of the bleachers, accepting meekly the adverse decisions of the men in blue, he would have grinned tolerantly. The Crab might mellow a little with advancing years, but lose his fighting spirit? Not in this world!

~~~~~~

It was in the spring of the following year when the team came straggling into camp for the annual conditioning process, and all but the Crab and one or two others had reported, that the Wolves were subjected to a severe jolt.

Rube Ferguson who had an eye for the dramatic waited until the gang was at morning batting practice. Then he broke the astounding news.

"The Crab's got himself a wife." The Wolves laughed.

"All right," said Ferguson, "all right—you fellows know it all; I'm a liar. The Crab's been married three months. I stood up with him. What's more, you fellows know the girl."

He took advantage of the general paralysis that followed this announcement to sneak up to the plate out of turn. He was still in there swinging when they came to life and rushed him. News is news, but a man's turn at bat, especially after an idle winter, is an inalienable right. Rube clung to his club.

"Three more cuts at the old apple," he bargained, "and I tell you who she is."

They fell back grumbling. Ferguson's last drive screamed into left field and whacked against the fence. Grinning contentedly he surrendered his bat and took his place at the end of the waiting line.

"Not so bad—I could have gone into third on that baby standing up. Trouble with you fellows is you're growing old. Now I—"

Brick McGovern raised a club menacingly. "Who'd the Crab marry?"

"Keep your shirt on," advised Ferguson. "I'm coming to that. It was the blonde at Steve's place."

"Not the Smile Girl?" The quick objection sprang from a dozen lips. "Not the little queen who sings—not the entertainer?"

Ferguson beamed happily. He had his sensation. "You said it," he told them. "The Smile Girl is now Mrs. Crab. She married Bill because the whole world was picking on him and it wasn't right. Ain't that a dame for you?"

They were inexpressibly shocked. The Smile Girl—daintiest wisp of cheer in the city—married to the Crab—surliest lump of gloom in baseball. The thing seemed incredible and yet—that was just the sort of girl she was—gravitating toward any one who was in distress. They swore in awed undertones. "What a bonehead play," sighed Boots Purnell, "what a Joe McGee! Imagine *any* one, let alone the Smile Girl, trying to live with the Crab! Give her an error—oh, give her six!" He made his sorrowful way to the plate, moaning over the appalling blunder.

Rube Ferguson's rich tenor sounded the opening lines of the Smile Girl's own song:

> "Smiling puts the blues to flight;
> Smiling makes each wrong come right—"

They joined mechanically in the chorus but they did not smile.

Pee-wee Patterson, midget second baseman, expressed what was in every one's mind:

"If anyone can tame the Crab, it's Goldilocks—but I'm betting she slips him his release by June. I wonder will he bring her to camp with him?"

The Crab settled this point himself the following day by showing up—alone and unchastened. He invited no questions and they forbore to offer any. He was as truculent and peevish as ever. The food was the bunk; someone had the room that he was entitled to; the bushers were too thick for comfort; the weather was "hell," and the new trainer didn't know a "charley horse" from a last year's bunion.

"The Crab's going to have a good year," observed Pee-wee, "twenty bucks says she gives him the gate by the first of June. Who wants it?"

Rube Ferguson whistled thoughtfully.

"If Brick will advance it to me I'll see you," he hazarded. "Some Janes are bears for punishment and the Crab ain't so worse. He made her quit her job and he staked her to a set of furniture and a flat. My wife says they're stuck on one another."

Pee-wee snorted. "Flypaper wouldn't stick to Bill after the first ten minutes." He raised his voice a little in imitation of Bull Feeney addressing the grandstand: "Batt'ries for today's game," he croaked, "the Smile Girl and the Crab. Bon soir, bye-bye, good night."

The Rube grinned. "Sure is a rummy battery," he agreed ruefully, "but the bet stands." He departed in search of McGovern and a piece of the bankroll.

Those of the Wolves who had not already met the Smile Girl, and they were mostly the rookies, learned to know her in the final days of the training season when the Wolves sought their home grounds for the polishing-up process.

She was enough of a child to want to accompany the Crab to the ball park for even the morning workouts and to say pretty things to each one individually. The Crab accomplished the introductions awkwardly, but it was evident that he was very proud of her and that she was very much in love with him. "Some guys have all the luck," lamented Boots Purnell. "If she ever benches the Crab, I'll be the first one to apply for his job."

At the opening game of the season, the Smile Girl's pink dress and picture hat were conspicuous in the front row of the grandstand just back of third base. Pink for happiness, she always said.

Rube Ferguson confided an important discovery to Brick McGovern and others between innings as they sat in the Wolf dugout.

"The Crab's keeping one eye on the batter and the other on his wife. I don't think he knows there's anybody else in the park. They've got a set of signals. Every time the Crab starts to splutter, she gives him the tip to lay off the rough stuff, and he chokes it back. Pee-wee, you lose!"

The diminutive second-sacker did not reply at once. He was searching wildly for his favorite stick. At length he found it and trotted off for his turn at the plate. He was back shortly, insisting loudly that the "last one was over his head."

"Now about the Crab," he confided to Rube, "everything's coming his way, get me? Wait until we hit the road for a while and the hot weather comes and the ace-in-the-hole boys get to working on him, then we'll see."

The Wolves, always a slow team to round to form because of the many veterans on the roster, trailed along in the second division and swung north in fifth place for their first extended road trip.

Gradually it became apparent to all that Peewee Patterson had called the turn on the Crab. He was plainly settling back into his old surly ways, snarling at the umpires, grumbling over the work of the pitchers, and demanding angrily that McGovern get someone behind the bat who didn't have a broken arm—this of Billy Hopper who could handcuff nine third basemen out of ten.

They were on the road four weeks and the Crab's batting average climbed steadily while his temper grew hourly worse. This was characteristic. He seemed able to vent considerable of his spite on the inoffensive leather. It was the nerves of his teammates that suffered.

"What did I tell you?" demanded Patterson, "now when we hit the home grounds next week—the Crab will get the panning of his life and the Smile Girl will break her heart over it. I tell you I'm calling the play!"

Brick McGovern and Rube Ferguson regarded their comrade-at-arms soberly. They felt that he spoke the truth.

"Well," commented Rube, "you can't bench a man that's hitting over .300 just to spare his wife's feelings." And with that understanding, the Crab was retained in the clean-up role.

Most ballplayers have a dislike for one or more cities on the circuit. The Crab's pet aversion was the St. Clair grounds. There, the huge double-decked grandstand, with its lower floor on a level with the infield itself and not forty feet from the foul lines, brought players and spectators into closer contact than was good for either. Back of the heavy screening and paralleling a well-worn path between the home plate and the dugout assigned to the home club, stretched "Sure Thing Row" where men who wagered money in downtown poolrooms before the game congregated like birds of prey to await the outcome.

"Sure Thing Row" ran to checked suits, diamonds and stacks of half dollars, the latter held lightly in one hand and riffled with the thumb and forefinger of the other. It broke no law of the land; it knew its rights and exercised every one of them.

"The Row" maintained a proprietary interest in the Crab. He was theirs by right of discovery. In him they recognized not only the strongest link in the Wolf defense but likewise the weakest. He was an unconscious instrument to be used or not as the odds might require. Now that the Crab was married, the problem was simplified.

It was in the third game of the series that Rube Ferguson, sitting beside Brick McGovern in the dugout while the Wolves were at bat, reported to his leader what was going on.

"The ace-in-the-hole boys are after the Crab. When he went up to bat just now they were whispering stuff to him about his wife—get me, Brick? They're handing him the laugh about the Smile Girl. He'll blow up before the inning's over."

McGovern nodded. His gnarled and sun-scorched hands opened and shut helplessly. "I know," he groaned, "I know—they used to hand it to me like that and if it hadn't been for my wife and kids I'd have done murder twenty times. There's no law against insulting a ballplayer. That goes with the price of admission. They'll not break the Crab's nerve but they'll get him thrown out. Ah!"

The gray-clad figures in the Wolf dugout sprang to their feet. The high-pitched yelp of the timber wolf pierced the clamor, followed by cries of "tear 'em, puppy!"

The Crab had lashed a terrific drive along the right field foul line and was rounding first base in full stride.

McGovern tore for the coaching box with both arms raised, palms outward. Walker in right field had knocked the drive down. He had one of the best arms in the league.

"None out," yelled the Wolf leader, "two bags—play it safe! Back—go back!"

But the Crab had eyes or ears for no one. He was running wild, bent only on showing "Sure Thing Row" he was its master. Blind with rage and excitement he bore down on third base. The ball zipped into the hands of the waiting fielder in plenty of time. The Crab must have known he was out, but he arose from a cloud of dust, wildly denunciatory, and frantic under the jibes of the bleachers and the foxfaced gentry back of the screen.

In the old belligerent way, he stalked after Tim Cahill and grabbed the umpire by the arm.

"You—you—" he foamed.

McGovern dashed out on the diamond but the mischief was already done. Cahill knew his business and he stood for no breach of discipline. Freeing himself from the Crab's clutch, he jerked a thumb in the direction of the clubhouse in center field.

"You're through for the day," he snapped, "off the field or I'll nick you for a ten-spot. Beat it!"

McGovern pulled his infielder away and shoved him in the direction indicated. "Don't be a fool, Bill," he advised, "you were out a mile."

The target for a storm of derisive hoots, the Crab made his way sullenly along the fence and into the clubhouse shadows. Not until he had vanished from sight did the last sibilant hiss die out.

McGovern walked back to the Wolves' pit and shot a quick glance at the Smile Girl sitting in her usual place just back of third. All around her, men were laughing at the Crab's discomfiture. She was smiling bravely but even at that distance he was certain that her chin was quivering.

"Sure Thing Row" settled back contentedly and winked. The Crab and his bludgeon had been eliminated from the crucial game of the series.

The Wolves lost by one run.

On the last day of June, just before the club left for another long swing around the circle, Rube Ferguson encountered little Patterson in front of the clubhouse. He drew the midget aside and handed him a twenty-dollar bill.

"Much obliged," acknowledged Pee-wee, "what's the idea?"

"The Crab's wife has left him."

"No!"

"Yes. She's been gone three days. She told my wife he came home and beefed because she was sewing something, and she said she could stand his crabbing about everything else but *that.*"

The second baseman looked incredulous.

"Seems like somebody's got their signals crossed, don't it? Why should that get her goat particularly? What was she sewing?"

The Rube shrugged. "What do women always sew? The money's yours."

The little infielder's eyes hardened. "I'm clean," he admitted. "I haven't got a red—but you put that twenty back in your pocket or I'll beat you to death."

Ferguson nodded his comprehension. "I feel that way about it, too. There's something likable about the Crab but I've never found out what it is. Will he be better or worse now?"

"Does a Crab ever change?" asked Pee-wee. During the next few weeks it seemed as though Patterson's question could admit of but one answer.

The Crab drew if anything a little closer into his shell. He was more morose, more savage in the clubhouse and on the diamond. He snarled his refusals when they offered him the usual hand of poker up in Boots Parnell's hotel room. When they left the clubhouse in the afternoons, he disappeared and they did not see him until the next morning. They forbore to question him. The ballplayer's code of ethics does not include discussion of domestic averages. While he continued to hit and field as he was doing, he was entitled to behave off the diamond in any way he saw fit.

Not until August when the club was in third place and going like a whirlwind, did the Crab give any indication that he missed the slim little figure in the pink dress who used to blow him kisses from the grandstand.

Then, so gradually that they had difficulty in comprehending the process, something under the Crab's shell began to disintegrate.

It was his hitting—that infallible barometer to a ballplayer's condition, that fell off first. Not that the Crab didn't connect just as frequently as ever, but his swings lacked the old driving power. Outfielders who used to back against the fence when he came up, now moved forward and had no trouble getting under the ball. From fourth place in the batting order he was dropped to sixth and then seventh without result. His huge shoulders seemed devitalized.

Next it was his fielding. He fumbled ground balls that ordinarily would have given him no trouble. He was slow on his feet and erratic in his throwing.

Jiggs Peterson, guardian of the right field pasture, called still another deficiency to the attention of the entire club one afternoon when, in a tight game with the Saints, a runner slid safely into third despite a perfect throw from deep right.

"I had that guy nailed by twenty feet," he complained to the Crab, "and you let him slide into the bag. What's the idea of taking the ball in back of the sack?"

The Crab's only reply was a mumbled, "You peg 'em right and I'll get 'em."

"Jiggs had called the turn," whispered Pee-wee, "the Crab is pulling away from the runner's spikes right along. I don't understand it."

"Nor I," Ferguson responded, "there was a time when he would have broken Jiggs in two for trying to call him like that."

The next day the Crab, seated beside his manager in the dugout, turned suddenly to McGovern.

"Brick—I can't find her—it's August and I can't find her."

McGovern masked his surprise. The Crab's eyes were bloodshot, the lines on his weather-beaten face sunk to unnatural depths. Several times McGovern opened his mouth but the right words did not occur to him.

"I can't find her," reiterated the Crab dully. "I lost her, and I can't find her."

McGovern scraped in the soft dirt with his cleats. He spoke as one man to another. "I'm sorry, Bill, I didn't know just how you felt about it."

The Crab contemplated the palm of a wornout glove. The muscles of his face twitched.

"I thought it was doll clothes she was sewing, Brick—she's such a kid. Honest to God I thought it was doll's clothes. I never knew different until I read her note. Now you know why I *got* to find her."

The pilot of the four-time pennant winners was again bereft of speech. He nodded slowly.

"She left no address," continued the third baseman. "She thought I was crabbing at her because—" his voice cracked sharply.

The Wolves came trooping noisily in from across the diamond. Their sorrel-topped pilot threw an arm carelessly around the Crab's shoulders.

"The Smile Girl couldn't hold a grudge against anyone," he whispered, "you'll hear from her one of these days. Why, man, any one could see she was nuts about you!"

The Crab's fingers closed on his leader's arm with a grip that made McGovern wince.

"You think so, Brick—on the level?"

"On the level, Bill."

That afternoon the Crab got two hits, the first he had negotiated in a week, but as the fifteenth of August approached, he slumped again, and McGovern benched him and made three unsuccessful attempts to bolster up the one weak spot in his infield. But good third basemen are not lying around loose in the middle of August. The Crab at his worst was better than the newcomers and McGovern put him back in the fray. Two of three major league scouts who had been attracted by the Crab's hitting and who had lingered in the hope that he would emerge from his slump, packed their grips and went elsewhere. The third man was a product of the school of McGraw. He studied the Crab through half-closed eyelids and—stayed.

With seven weeks of the season still unplayed, the Wolves returned from a southern trip in second place. The fine lines of worry between McGovern's eyes deepened. He caught himself watching the apathetic figure of the Crab and praying that the third baseman would regain just a little of his old fighting spirit.

And then one afternoon just before the umpire called the Wolves and Tigers together for the opening game of the week, Rube Ferguson, idol of the right field bleachers, tossed a number of neatly folded newspapers into the pit.

"Compliments of 'Pebble Pop,' champion groundkeeper of the world," he told them, "pipe the writeup they gave the old boy."

The Crab opened his paper listlessly, glanced over the tribute to the veteran caretaker, and permitted the pages to slip to the concrete floor of the dugout. He was in the act of thrusting the paper aside with his cleats, when his eye caught a single word in blackface type up near the top of the column on the reverse side of the sporting page. It was his own name. Hypnotically, he picked up the page and stared at it. The words that followed the black-faced capitals burned themselves into his brain.

A sharp ejaculation caused McGovern to look up. The Crab's teeth were chattering.

"What's wrong?"

"N-n-nothing," stammered the Crab. The paper rustled from his nerveless hands. He straightened up, looked around wildly and then walked up and out of the pit—straight as a chalk line to the exit back of first base. With the entire team watching him, openmouthed, the Crab wrenched savagely at the gate. A special officer drew the bolt, and the third baseman disappeared into the crowd, uniform and all.

Pee-wee Patterson broke the silence.

"I knew it was coming. He's cuckoo. Somebody better follow him."

But Brick McGovern was scanning the paper that the third baseman had dropped.

"Cuckoo, nothing," he exclaimed, "the Crab has found his wife!"

They all saw it then—two lines of agate type that began: "CROW-LEY—"

The paper was eight days old.

~~~~~~

A sorrel-topped Irishman with a fighting face, but rather too generous about the middle for perfect condition, plodded up the steps of St. Joseph's Hospital at dusk. One hand grasped a bouquet of pink roses.

"Ah, yes," said the little woman in the office, "second floor of the Annex—Room 41."

McGovern located the room and tapped gently on the white door.

"Come in," chirped a voice.

The pilot of the Wolves turned the knob dubiously and peered into the room.

The Smile Girl was sitting up in bed. Her eyes were bright with the look that comes to a woman who has borne her mate his first man-child. She beckoned to McGovern and then held a pink finger to her lips.

"S-sh!" she whispered, "look!"

In an armchair facing the window and away from the door, McGovern made out a familiar figure, still in uniform. It was rocking gently back and forth, cleats tapping on the linoleum-covered floor, and as it rocked it sang most unmusically to a rose-colored bundle held awkwardly over one shoulder:

"Smile awhile—and I'll smile, too, What's the good of feeling blue?
Watch my lips—I'll show you how:
That's the way—you're smiling now!"

McGovern blew his nose. The singing stopped abruptly.

"Honey," said the Smile Girl, "bring William, Junior, to me. You've had him for most an hour and I want to show him to Mr. McGovern."

The Crab's cleats click-clacked across the room. He held up the bundle for McGovern's inspection.

"I'd let you hold him, Brick," he confided, "but it's got to be done just a certain way. The nurse put me wise; see—you keep one hand back of the neck and shoulders, so you don't do no fumbling."

McGovern nodded. He deposited the roses on the bed and laid the tip of one pudgy finger ever so lightly on the cheek of the sleeping infant.

"Some kid," he marveled, *"some kid!"*

The Smile Girl emitted a cry of surprise. From an envelope attached to the roses she had extracted a hundred-dollar bill.

"What's that?" demanded the Crab crossly, "what you trying to put over, Brick? I haven't touched a bean of my salary for three months. I don't need—"

"Shut up!" admonished McGovern. "Can't I take an option on the little fellow's services if I want to? Look at those hands, Bill—ain't they made for an infielder—they're yours all over—he's got your eyes and your hair and—"

The baby squirmed and moved its hands restlessly. The lusty wail of a perfectly healthy and hungry man-cub brought a nurse hurrying into the room.

With obvious reluctance, Bill Crowley surrendered his possession. He brushed one hand hastily across his eyes.

"Darn little crab," he said huskily, "he *does* look like me just a little bit, *don't* he, Brick?"

~~~~~~

Digger Grimes, base runner par excellence, flashed past first and second in an ever-widening circle and headed for third. He was well between the two bags when Pee-wee Patterson, crouched in short center, took the throw from his old and esteemed friend Rube Ferguson and with a single motion shot the ball, low and a trifle wide of the waiting figure at third.

It was the seventh inning of the last game of the season. Thirty thousand fans in bleachers and grandstand rose to their feet. The play was close, so close that men forgot to breathe. Twenty feet from the bag, the runner made his leap. Spikes flashed in the sunlight menacingly. The Digger was corning in at an angle opposite to the guardian of the bag charging with his fangs bared!

At the same instant, a heavy-shouldered figure in the familiar uniform of the champion Wolves swept up the ball with one bare hand and flung himself headlong in the path of the plunging runner. The two figures thudded together—threshed a moment in a flurry of arms and legs and then were still.

With his cleats still six inches from the bag, Digger Grimes found himself pinned to the dirt under 180 pounds of inexorable bone and muscle.

Out from a cloud of dust, while the bleachers and grandstand rocked in a tempest of glee, came an indignant bellow:

"He's out—I tell you!—he ain't touched the bag yet—he's out!"

The Crab catapulted to his feet and advanced on Dan McLaughlin. The umpire turned mild blue eyes on the Wolf infielder.

"I called him out," he protested, "what do you want—a written notice?"

The Crab blinked a moment, and stalked back to his position. From under the visor of his cap he shot a swift glance at the crowded benches just back of third. A blur of pink and a smaller blur of blue showed up against the dark background of masculine fandom and told him all he wished to know.

The Crab's chest expanded, as is only proper when a man has got his two hits. Pounding the palm of his worn glove, he dug his cleats into the dirt and set himself for the next play.

"Come on," he called, "get the next man! Ump—it's too bad you only got one lung—can't call a play louder than a whisper, can you? Pipes all rusty, huh? Too bad!"

Over in the Wolf dugout, a red-headed manager who had seen his club climb into the lead in the closing days of the grueling struggle, smiled faintly and stared with unseeing eyes across the diamond. His fingers twisted a telegram that had come to him that morning from New York.

Ten thousand dollars cash and spring delivery is too tempting an offer for any minor-league manager to reject. But there would be a wide hole at third base next year, and Brick McGovern was already wondering how he would ever plug it.

MY ROOMY

RING LARDNER

I

No—I ain't signed for next year; but there won't be no trouble about that. The dough part of it is all fixed up. John and me talked it over and I'll sign as soon as they send me a contract. All I told him was that he'd have to let me pick my own roommate after this and not sick no wild man on to me.

You know I didn't hit much the last two months o' the season. Some o' the boys, I notice, wrote some stuff about me gettin' old and losin' my battin' eye. That's all bunk! The reason I didn't hit was because I wasn't gettin' enough sleep. And the reason for that was Mr. Elliott.

He wasn't with us after the last part o' May, but I roomed with him long enough to get the insomny. I was the only guy in the club game enough to stand for him; but I was sorry afterward that I done it, because it sure did put a crimp in my little old average.

And do you know where he is now? I got a letter today and I'll read it to you. No—I guess I better tell you somethin' about him first. You fellers never got acquainted with him and you ought to hear the dope to understand the letter. I'll make it as short as I can.

He didn't play in no league last year. He was with some semipros over in Michigan and somebody writes John about him. So John sends Needham over to look at him. Tom stayed there Saturday and Sunday, and seen him work twice. He was playin' the outfield, but as luck would have it they wasn't a fly ball hit in his direction in both games. A base hit was made out his way and he booted it, and that's the only report Tom could get on his fieldin'. But he wallops two over the wall in one day and they catch two line drives off him. The next day he gets four blows and two o' them is triples.

So Tom comes back and tells John the guy is a whale of a hitter and fast as Cobb, but he don't know nothin' about his fieldin'. Then John signs him to a contract—twelve hundred or somethin' like that. We'd been in Tampa a week before he showed up. Then he comes to the hotel and just sits round all day, without tellin' nobody who he was. Finally the bellhops was going to chase him out and he says he's one o' the ballplayers. Then the clerk gets John to go over and talk to him. He tells John his name and says he hasn't had nothin' to eat for three days, because he was broke. John told me afterward that he'd drew about three hundred in advance—last winter sometime. Well, they took him in the dinin' room and they tell me he inhaled about four meals at once. That night they roomed him with Heine.

Next mornin' Heine and me walks out to the grounds together and Heine tells me about him. He says:

"Don't never call me a bug again. They got me roomin' with the champion o' the world."

"Who is he?" I says.

"I don't know and I don't want to know," says Heine; "but if they stick him in there with me again I'll jump to the Federals. To start with, he ain't got no baggage. I ast him where his trunk was and he says he didn't have none. Then I ast him if he didn't have no suitcase, and he says: 'No. What do you care?' I was goin' to lend him some pajamas, but he put on the shirt o' the uniform John gave him last night and slept in that. He was asleep when I got up this mornin'. I seen his collar layin' on the dresser and it looked like he had wore it in Pittsburgh every day for a year. So I throwed it out the window and he comes down to breakfast with no collar. I ast him what size collar he wore and he says he didn't want none, because he wasn't goin' out nowheres. After breakfast he beat it up to the room again and put on his uniform. When I got up there he was lookin' in the glass at himself, and he done it all the time I was dressin'."

When we got out to the park I got my first look at him. Pretty good-lookin' guy, too, in his unie—big shoulders and well put together; built somethin' like Heine himself. He was talkin' to John when I come up.

"What position do you play?" John was askin' him.

"I play anywheres," says Elliott.

"You're the kind I'm lookin' for," says John. Then he says: "You was an outfielder up there in Michigan, wasn't you?"

"I don't care where I play," says Elliott.

John sends him to the outfield and forgets all about him for a while. Pretty soon Miller comes in and says:

"I ain't goin' to shag for no bush outfielder!"

John ast him what was the matter, and Miller tells him that Elliott ain't doin' nothin' but just standin' out there; that he ain't makin' no attemp' to catch the fungoes, and that he won't even chase 'em. Then John starts watchin' him, and it was just like Miller said. Larry hit one pretty near in his lap and he stepped out o' the way. John calls him in and ast him:

"Why don't you go after them fly balls?"

"Because I don't want 'em," says Elliott. John gets sarcastic and says:

"What do you want? Of course we'll see that you get anythin' you want!"

"Give me a ticket back home," says Elliott. "Don't you want to stick with the club?" says John, and the busher tells him, no, he certainly did not. Then John tells him he'll have to pay his own fare home and Elliott don't get sore at all. He just says:

"Well, I'll have to stick, then—because I'm broke."

We was havin' battin' practice and John tells him to go up and hit a few. And you ought to of seen him bust 'em!

Lavender was in there workin' and he'd been pitchin' a little all winter, so he was in pretty good shape. He lobbed one up to Elliott, and he hit it 'way up in some trees outside the fence—about a mile, I guess. Then John tells Jimmy to put somethin' on the ball. Jim comes through with one of his fast ones and the kid slams it agin the right-field wall on a line.

"Give him your spitter!" yells John, and Jim handed him one. He pulled it over first base so fast that Bert, who was standin' down there, couldn't hardly duck in time. If it'd hit him it'd killed him.

Well, he kep' on hittin' everythin' Jim give him and Jim had somethin' too. Finally John gets Pierce warmed up and sends him out to pitch, tellin' him to hand Elliott a flock o' curve balls. He wanted to see if lefthanders was goin' to bother him. But he slammed 'em right along, and I don't b'lieve he hit more'n two the whole mornin' that wouldn't of been base hits in a game.

They sent him out to the outfield again in the afternoon, and after a lot o' coaxin' Leach got him to go after fly balls; but that's all he did do—just go after 'em. One hit him on the bean and another on the shoulder. He run back after the short ones and 'way in after the ones that went over his head. He catched just one—a line drive that he couldn't get out o' the way of; and then he acted like it hurt his hands.

I come back to the hotel with John. He ast me what I thought of Elliott.

"Well," I says, "he'd be the greatest ballplayer in the world if he could just play ball. He sure can bust 'em."

John says he was afraid he couldn't never make an outfielder out o' him. He says:

"I'll try him on the infield to-morrow. They must be some place he can play. I never seen a lefthand hitter that looked so good agin lefthand pitchin'—and he's got a great arm; but he acts like he'd never saw a fly ball."

Well, he was just as bad on the infield. They put him at short and he was like a sieve. You could of drove a hearse between him and second base without him gettin' near it. He'd stoop over for a ground ball about the time it was bouncin' up agin the fence; and when he'd try to cover the bag on a peg he'd trip over it.

They tried him at first base and sometimes he'd run 'way over in the coachers' box and sometimes out in right field lookin' for the bag. Once Heine shot one acrost at him on a line and he never touched it with his hands. It went barn! right in the pit of his stomach—and the lunch he'd ate didn't do him no good.

Finally John just give up and says he'd have to keep him on the bench and let him earn his pay by bustin' 'em a couple o' times a week or so. We all agreed with John that this bird would be a whale of a pinch hitter—and we was right too. He was hittin' 'way over five hundred when the blowoff come, along about the last o' May.

II

Before the trainin' trip was over, Elliott had roomed with pretty near everybody in the club. Heine raised an awful holler after the second night down there and John put the bug in with Needham. Tom stood him for three nights. Then he doubled up with Archer, and Schulte, and Miller, and Leach, and Saier—and the whole bunch in turn, averagin' about two nights with each one before they put up a kick. Then John tried him with some o' youngsters, but they wouldn't stand for him no more'n the others. They all said he was crazy and they was afraid he'd get violent some night and stick a knife in 'em. He always insisted on havin' the water run in the bathtub all night, because he said it reminded him of the sound of the dam near his home. The fellers might get up four or five times a night and shut off the faucet, but he'd get right up after 'em and turn it on again. Carter, a big bush pitcher from Georgia, started a fight with him about it one night, and Elliott pretty near killed him. So the rest o' the bunch, when they'd saw Carter's map next mornin', didn't have the nerve to do nothin' when it come their turn.

Another o' his habits was the thing that scared 'em, though. He'd brought a razor with him—in his pocket, I guess—and he used to do his shavin' in the middle o' the night. Instead o' doin' it in the bathroom he'd lather his face and then come out and stand in front o' the lookin' glass on the dresser. Of course he'd have all the lights turned on, and that was bad enough when a feller wanted to sleep; but the worst of it was that he'd stop shavin' every little while and turn round and stare at the guy who was makin' a failure o' tryin' to sleep. Then he'd wave his razor round in the air and laugh, and begin shavin' agin. You can imagine how comf'table his roomies felt!

John had bought him a suitcase and some clothes and things, and charged 'em up to him. He'd drew so much dough in advance that he didn't have nothin' comin' till about June. He never thanked John and he'd wear one shirt and one collar till some one throwed 'em away.

Well, we finally gets to Indianapolis, and we was goin' from there to Cincy to open. The last day in Indianapolis John come and ast me how I'd like to change roomies. I says I was perfectly satisfied with Larry. Then John says:

"I wisht you'd try Elliott. The other boys all kicks on him, but he seems to hang round you a lot and I b'lieve you could get along all right."

"Why don't you room him alone?" I ast.

"The boss or the hotels won't stand for us roomin' alone," says John. "You go ahead and try it, and see how you make out. If he's too much for you let me know; but he likes you and I think he'll be diff'rent with a guy who can talk to him like you can."

So I says I'd tackle it, because I didn't want to throw John down. When we got to Cincy they stuck Elliott and me in one room, and we was together till he quit us.

III

I went to the room early that night, because we was goin' to open next day and I wanted to feel like somethin'. First thing I done when I got undressed was turn on both faucets in the bathtub. They was makin' an awful racket when Elliott finally come in about midnight. I was layin' awake and I opened right up on him. I says:

"Don't shut off that water, because I like to hear it run."

Then I turned over and pretended to be asleep. The bug got his clothes off, and then what did he do but go in the bathroom and shut off the water! Then he come back in the room and says:

"I guess no one's goin' to tell me what to do in here."

But I kep' right on pretendin' to sleep and didn't pay no attention. When he'd got into his bed I jumped out o' mine and turned on all the lights and begun stroppin' my razor. He says:

"What's comin' off?"

"Some o' my whiskers," I says. "I always shave along about this time."

"No, you don't!" he says. "I was in your room one mornin' down in Louisville and I seen you shavin' then."

"Well," I says, "the boys tell me you shave in the middle o' the night; and I thought if I done all the things you do mebbe I'd get so's I could hit like you."

"You must be superstitious!" he says. And I told him I was.

"I'm a good hitter," he says, "and I'd be a good hitter if I never shaved at all. That don't make no diff'rence."

"Yes, it does," I says. "You prob'ly hit good because you shave at night; but you'd be a better fielder if you shaved in the mornin'."

You see, I was tryin' to be just as crazy as him though that wasn't hardly possible.

"If that's right," says he, "I'll do my shavin' in the mornin'—because I seen in the papers where the boys says that if I could play the outfield like I can hit I'd be as good as Cobb. They tell me Cobb gets twenty thousand a year."

"No," I says; "he don't get that much—but he gets about ten times as much as you do."

"Well," he says, "I'm goin' to be as good as him, because I need the money."

"What do you want with money?" I says.

He just laughed and didn't say nothin'; but from that time on the water didn't run in the bathtub nights and he done his shavin' after breakfast. I didn't notice, though, that he looked any better in fieldin' practice.

I V

It rained one day in Cincy and they trimmed us two out o' the other three; but it wasn't Elliott's fault. They had Larry beat four to one in the ninth innin' o' the first game. Archer gets on with two out, and John sends my roomy up to hit—though Benton, a lefthander, is workin' for them. The first thing Benton serves up there Elliott cracks it a mile over Hobby's head. It would of been good for three easy— only Archer—playin' safe, o' course—pulls up at third base. Tommy couldn't do nothin' and we was licked.

The next day he hits one out o' the park off the Indian; but we was 'way behind and they was nobody on at the time. We copped the last one without usin' no pinch hitters.

I didn't have no trouble with him nights durin' the whole series. He come to bed pretty late while we was there and I told him he'd better not let John catch him at it.

"What would he do?" he says. "Fine you fifty," I says.

"He can't fine me a dime," he says, "because I ain't got it."

Then I told him he'd be fined all he had comin' if he didn't get in the hotel before midnight; but he just laughed and says he didn't think John had a kick comin' so long as he kep' bustin' the ball.

"Some day you'll go up there and you won't bust it," I says.

"That'll be an accident," he says.

That stopped me and I didn't say nothin'. What could you say to a guy who hated himself like that?

The "accident" happened in St. Louis the first day. We needed two runs in the eighth and Saier and Brid was on, with two out. John tells Elliott to go up in Pierce's place. The bug goes up and Griner gives him two bad balls—'way outside. I thought they was goin' to walk him—and it looked like good judgment, because they'd heard what he done in Cincy. But no! Griner comes back with a fast one right over and Elliott pulls it down the right foul line, about two foot foul. He hit it so hard you'd of thought they'd sure walk him then; but Griner gives him another fast one. He slammed it again just as hard, but foul. Then Griner gives him one 'way outside and it's two and three. John says, on the bench:

"If they don't walk him now he'll bust that fence down."

I thought the same and I was sure Griner wouldn't give him nothin' to hit; but he come with a curve and Rigler calls Elliott out. From where we sat the last one looked low, and I thought Elliott'd make a kick. He come back to the bench smilin'.

John starts for his position, but stopped and ast the bug what was the matter with that one. Any busher I ever knowed would of said, "It was too low," or "It was outside," or "It was inside." Elliott says:

"Nothin' at all. It was right over the middle."

"Why didn't you bust it, then?" says John.

"I was afraid I'd kill somebody," says Elliott, and laughed like a big boob.

John was pretty near chokin'. "What are you laughin' at?" he says.

"I was thinkin' of a nickel show I seen in Cincinnati," says the bug.

"Well," says John, so mad he couldn't hardly see, "that show and that laugh'll cost you fifty."

We got beat, and I wouldn't of blamed John if he'd fined him his whole season's pay.

Up 'n the room that night I told him he'd better cut out that laughin' stuff when we was gettin' trimmed or he never would have no pay day. Then he got confidential.

"Pay day wouldn't do me no good," he says. "When I'm all squared up with the club and begin to have a pay day, I'll only get a hundred bucks at a time, and I'll owe that to some o' you fellers. I wisht we could win the pennant and get in on that World's Series dough. Then I'd get a bunch at once."

"What would you do with a bunch o' dough?" I ast him.

"Don't tell nobody, sport," he says; "but if I ever get five hundred at once I'm goin' to get married."

"Oh!" I says. "And who's the lucky girl?"

"She's a girl up in Muskegon," says Elliott; "and you're right when you call her lucky."

"You don't like yourself much, do you?" I says.

"I got reason to like myself," says he. "You'd like yourself, too if you could hit 'em like me."

"Well," I says, "you didn't show me no hittin' to-day."

"I couldn't hit because I was laughin' too hard," says Elliott.

"What was it you was laughin' at?" I says.

"I was laughin' at that pitcher," he says. "He thought he had somethin' and he didn't have nothin'."

"He had enough to whiff you with," I says.

"He didn't have nothin'!" says he again. "I was afraid if I busted one off him they'd can him, and then I couldn't never hit agin him no more."

Naturally I didn't have no comeback to that. I just sort o' gasped and got ready to go to sleep; but he wasn't through.

"I wisht you could see this bird!" he says.

"What bird?" I says.

"This dame that's nuts about me," he says.

"Good-looker?" I ast.

"No," he says; "she ain't no bear for looks. They ain't nothin' about her for a guy to rave over till you hear her sing. She sure can holler some."

"What kind o' voice has she got?" I ast.

"A bear," says he.

"No," I says; "I mean is she a barytone or an air?"

"I don't know," he says; "but she's got the loudest voice I ever hear on a woman. She's pretty near got me beat."

"Can you sing?" I says; and I was sorry right afterward that I ast him that question.

I guess it must of been bad enough to have the water runnin' night after night and to have him wavin' that razor round; but that couldn't of been nothin' to his singin'. Just as soon as I'd pulled that boner he says, "Listen to me!" and starts in on 'Silver Threads Among the Gold.' Mind you, it was after midnight and they was guests all round us tryin' to sleep!

They used to be noise enough in our club when we had Hofman and Sheckard and Richie harmonizin'; but this bug's voice was louder'n all o' theirn combined. We once had a pitcher named Martin Walsh—brother o' Big Ed's—and I thought he could drownd out the Subway; but this guy made a boiler factory sound like Dummy Taylor. If the whole hotel wasn't awake when he'd howled the first line it's a pipe they was when he cut loose, which he done when he come to "Always young and fair to me." Them words could of been heard easy in East St. Louis.

He didn't get no encore from me, but he goes right through it again—or starts to. I knowed somethin' was goin' to happen before he finished—and somethin' did. The night clerk and the house detective come bangin' at the door. I let 'em in and they had plenty to say. If we made another sound the whole club'd be canned out o' the hotel. I tried to salve 'em, and I says:

"He won't sing no more."

But Elliott swelled up like a poisoned pup.

"Won't I?" he says. "I'll sing all I want to."

"You won't sing in here," says the clerk.

"They ain't room for my voice in here anyways," he says. "I'll go outdoors and sing."

And he puts his clothes on and ducks out. I didn't make no attemp' to stop him. I heard him bellowin' 'Silver Threads' down the corridor and down the stairs, with the clerk and the dick chasin' him all the way and tellin' him to shut up.

Well, the guests make a holler the next mornin'; and the hotel people tells Charlie Williams that he'll either have to let Elliott stay somewheres else or the whole club'll have to move. Charlie tells John, and John was thinkin' o' settlin' the question by releasin' Elliott.

I guess he'd about made up his mind to do it; but that afternoon they had us three to one in the ninth, and we got the bases full, with two down and Larry's turn to hit. Elliott had been sittin' on the bench sayin' nothin'.

"Do you think you can hit one today?" says John.

"I can hit one any day," says Elliott.

"Go up and hit that lefthander, then," says John, "and remember there's nothin' to laugh at."

Sallee was workin'—and workin' good; but that didn't bother the bug. He cut into one, and it went between Oakes and Whitted like a shot. He come into third standin' up and we was a run to the good. Sallee was so sore he kind o' forgot himself and took pretty near his full wind-up pitchin' to Tommy. And what did Elliott do but steal home and get away with it clean!

Well, you couldn't can him after that, could you? Charlie gets him a room somewheres and I was relieved of his company that night. The next evenin' we beat it for Chi to play about two weeks at home. He didn't tell nobody where he roomed there and I didn't see nothin' of him, 'cep' out to the park. I ast him what he did with himself nights and he says:

"Same as I do on the road—borrow some dough some place and go to the nickel shows."

"You must be stuck on 'em," I says.

"Yes," he says; "I like the ones where they kill people—because I want to learn how to do it. I may have that job some day."

"Don't pick on me," I says.

"Oh," says the bug, "you never can tell who I'll pick on."

It seemed as if he just couldn't learn nothin' about fieldin', and finally John told him to keep out o' the practice.

"A ball might hit him in the temple and croak him," says John.

But he busted up a couple o' games for us at home, beatin' Pittsburgh once and Cincy once.

V

They give me a great big room at the hotel in Pittsburgh; so the fellers picked it out for the poker game. We was playin' along about ten o'clock one night when in come Elliott—the earliest he'd showed up since we'd been roomin' together. They was only five of us playin' and Tom ast him to sit in.

"I'm busted," he says.

"Can you play poker?" I ast him.

"They's nothin' I can't do!" he says. "Slip me a couple o' bucks and I'll show you."

So I slipped him a couple o' bucks and honestly hoped he'd win, because I knowed he never had no dough. Well, Tom dealt him a hand and he picks it up and says:

"I only got five cards."

"How many do you want?" I says.

"Oh," he says, "if that's all I get I'll try to make 'em do."

The pot was cracked and raised, and he stood the raise. I says to myself: "There goes my two bucks!" But no—he comes out with three queens and won the dough. It was only about seven bucks; but you'd of thought it was a million to see him grab it. He laughed like a kid.

"Guess I can't play this game!" he says; and he had me fooled for a minute—I thought he must of been kiddin' when he complained of only havin' five cards.

He copped another pot right afterward and was sittin' there with about eleven bucks in front of him when Jim opens a roodle pot for a buck. I stays and so does Elliott. Him and Jim both drawed one card and I took three. I had kings or queens—I forget which. I didn't help 'em none; so when Jim bets a buck I throws my hand away.

"How much can I bet?" says the bug.

"You can raise Jim a buck if you want to," I says.

So he bets two dollars. Jim comes back at him. He comes right back at Jim. Jim raises him again and he tilts Jim right back. Well, when he'd boosted Jim with the last buck he had, Jim says:

"I'm ready to call. I guess you got me beat. What have you got?"

"I know what I've got, all right," says Elliott. "I've got a straight." And he throws his hand down. Sure enough, it was a straight, eight high. Jim pretty near fainted and so did I.

The bug had started pullin' in the dough when Jim stops him.

"Here! Wait a minute!" says Jim. "I thought you had somethin'. I filled up." Then Jim lays down his nine full.

"You beat me, I guess," says Elliott, and he looked like he'd lost his last friend.

"Beat you?" says Jim. "Of course I beat you! What did you think I had?"

"Well," says the bug. "I thought you might have a small flush or somethin'."

When I regained consciousness he was beggin' for two more bucks.

"What for?" I says. "To play poker with? You're barred from the game for life!"

"Well," he says, "if I can't play no more I want to go to sleep, and you fellers will have to get out o' this room."

Did you ever hear o' nerve like that? This was the first night he'd came in before twelve and he orders the bunch out so's he can sleep! We politely suggested to him to go to Brooklyn.

Without sayin' a word he starts in on his 'Silver Threads'; and it wasn't two minutes till the game was busted up and the bunch—all but me—was out o' there. I'd of beat it too, only he stopped yellin' as soon as they'd went.

"You're some buster!" I says. "You bust up ball games in the afternoon and poker games at night."

"Yes," he says; "that's my business—bustin' things."

And before I knowed what he was about he picked up the pitcher of ice-water that was on the floor and throwed it out the window—through the glass and all.

Right then I give him a plain talkin' to. I tells him how near he come to gettin' canned down in St. Louis because he raised so much Cain singin' in the hotel.

"But I had to keep my voice in shape," he says. "If I ever get dough enough to get married the girl and me'll go out singin' together."

"Out where?" I ast.

"Out on the vaudeville circuit," says Elliot.

"Well," I says, "if her voice is like yours you'll be wastin' money if you travel round. Just stay up in Muskegon and we'll hear you, all right!"

I told him he wouldn't never get no dough if he didn't behave himself. That, even if we got in the World's Series, he wouldn't be with us—unless he cut out the foolishness.

"We ain't goin' to get in no World's Series," he says, "and I won't never get a bunch o' money at once; so it looks like I couldn't get married this fall." Then I told him we played a city series every fall. He'd never thought o' that and it tickled him to death. I told him the losers always got about five hundred apiece and that we were about due to win it and get about eight hundred. "But," I says, "we still got a good chance for the old pennant; and if I was you I wouldn't give up hope o' that yet—not where John can hear you, anyway."

"No," he says, "we won't win no pennant, because he won't let me play reg'lar; but I don't care so long as we're sure o' that city-series dough."

"You ain't sure of it if you don't behave," I says.

"Well," says he, very serious, "I guess I'll behave."

And he did—till we made our first Eastern trip.

VI

We went to Boston first, and that crazy bunch goes out and piles up a three-run lead on us in seven innin's the first day. It was the pitcher's turn to lead off in the eighth, so up goes Elliot to bat for him. He kisses the first thing they hands him for three bases; and we says, on the bench: "Now we'll get 'em!"because, you know, a three-run lead wasn't nothin' in Boston.

"Stay right on that bag!" John hollers to Elliott. Mebbe if John hadn't said nothin' to him every thin' would of been all right; but when Perdue starts to pitch the first ball to Tommy, Elliott starts to steal home. He's out as far as from here to Seattle.

If I'd been carryin' a gun I'd of shot him right through the heart. As it was, I thought John'd kill him with a bat, because he was standin' there with a couple of 'em, waitin' for his turn; but I guess John was too stunned to move. He didn't even seem to see Elliott when he went to the bench. After I'd cooled off a little I says:

"Beat it and get into your clothes before John comes in. Then go to the hotel and keep out o' sight."

When I got up in the room afterward, there was Elliott, lookin' as innocent and happy as though he'd won fifty bucks with a pair o' treys.

"I thought you might of killed yourself," I says.

"What for?" he says.

"For that swell play you made," says I.

"What was the matter with the play?" ast Elliott, surprised. "It was all right when I done it in St. Louis."

"Yes," I says; "but they was two out in St. Louis and we wasn't no three runs behind."

"Well," he says, "if it was all right in St. Louis I don't see why it was wrong here."

"It's a diff'rent climate here," I says, too disgusted to argue with him.

"I wonder if they'd let me sing in this climate?" says Elliott.

"No," I says. "Don't sing in this hotel, because we don't want to get fired out o' here—the eats is too good."

"All right," he says. "I won't sing." But when I starts down to supper he says: "I'm li'ble to do somethin' worse'n sing."

He didn't show up in the dinin' room and John went to the boxin' show after supper; so it looked like him and Elliott wouldn't run into each other till the murder had left John's heart. I was glad o' that because a Mass'chusetts jury might not consider it justifiable hom-mercide if one guy croaked another for givin' the Boston club a game.

I went down to the corner and had a couple o' beers; and then I came straight back, intendin' to hit the hay. The elevator boy had went for a drink or somethin', and they was two old ladies already waitin' in the car when I stepped in. Right along after me comes Elliott.

"Where's the boy that's supposed to run this car?" he says. I told him the boy'd be right back; but he says: "I can't wait. I'm much too sleepy."

And before I could stop him he'd slammed the door and him and I and the poor old ladies was shootin' up.

"Let us off at the third floor, please!" says one o' the ladies, her voice kind o' shakin'.

"Sorry, madam," says the bug; "but this is a express and we don't stop at no third floor."

I grabbed his arm and tried to get him away from the machinery; but he was as strong as a ox and he throwed me agin the side o' the car like I was a baby. We went to the top faster'n I ever rode in an eleva-tor before. And then we shot down to the bottom, hittin' the bumper down there so hard I thought we'd be smashed to splinters.

The ladies was too scared to make a sound durin' the first trip; but while we was goin' up and down the second time—even faster'n the first—they begun to scream. I was hollerin' my head off at him to quit and he was makin' more noise than the three of us—pretendin' he was the locomotive and the whole crew o' the train.

Don't never ask me how many times we went up and down! The women fainted on the third trip and I guess I was about as near it as I'll ever get. The elevator boy and the bellhops and the waiters and the night clerk and everybody was jumpin' round the lobby screamin'; but no one seemed to know how to stop us.

Finally—on about the tenth trip, I guess—he slowed down and stopped at the fifth floor, where we was roomin'. He opened the door and beat it for the room, while I, though I was tremblin' like a leaf, run the car down to the bottom.

The night clerk knowed me pretty well and knowed I wouldn't do nothin' like that; so him and I didn't argue, but just got to work together to bring the old women to. While we was doin' that Elliott must of run down the stairs and slipped out o' the hotel, because when they sent the officers up to the room after him he'd blowed.

They was goin' to fire the club out; but Charlie had a good stand-in with Amos, the proprietor, and he fixed it up to let us stay—providin' Elliott kep' away. The bug didn't show up at the ball park next day and we didn't see no more of him till we got on the rattler for New York. Charlie and John both bawled him, but they give him a berth—an upper and we pulled into the Grand Central Station without him havin' made no effort to wreck the train.

VII

I'd studied the thing pretty careful, but hadn't come to no conclusion. I was sure he wasn't no stew, because none o' the boys had ever saw him even take a glass o' beer, and I couldn't never detect the odor o' booze on him. And if he'd been a dope I'd of knew about it—roomin' with him.

There wouldn't of been no mystery about it if he'd been a left-hand pitcher—but he wasn't. He wasn't nothin' but a whale of a hitter and he throwed with his right arm. He hit lefthanded, o' course; but so did Saier and Brid and Schulte and me, and John himself; and none of us was violent. I guessed he must of been just a plain nut and li'ble to break out any time.

They was a letter waitin' for him at New York, and I took it, intendin' to give it to him at the park, because I didn't think they'd let him room at the hotel; but after breakfast he come up to the room, with his suitcase. It seems he'd promised John and Charlie to be good, and made it so strong they b'lieved him.

I give him his letter, which was addressed in a girl's writin' and come from Muskegon.

"From the girl?" I says.

"Yes," he says; and, without openin' it, he tore it up and throwed it out the window.

"Had a quarrel?" I ast.

"No, no," he says; "but she can't tell me nothin' I don't know already. Girls always writes the same junk. I got one from her in Pittsburgh, but I didn't read it."

"I guess you ain't so stuck on her," I says. He swells up and says:

"Of course I'm stuck on her! If I wasn't, do you think I'd be goin' round with this bunch and gettin' insulted all the time? I'm stickin' here because o' that series dough, so's I can get hooked."

"Do you think you'd settle down if you was married?" I ast him.

"Settle down?" he says. "Sure, I'd settle down. I'd be so happy that I wouldn't have to look for no excitement."

Nothin' special happened that night 'cep' that he come in the room about one o'clock and woke me up by pickin' up the foot o' the bed and dropping it on the floor, sudden-like.

"Give me a key to the room," he says.

"You must of had a key," I says, "or you couldn't of got in."

"That's right!" he says, and beat it to bed.

One o' the reporters must of told Elliott that John had ast for waivers on him and New York had refused to waive, because next mornin' he come to me with that dope.

"New York's goin' to win this pennant!" he says. "Well," I says, "they will if some one else don't.

But what of it?"

"I'm goin' to play with New York," he says, "so's I can get the World's Series dough."

"How you goin' to get away from this club?" I ast.

"Just watch me!" he says. "I'll be with New York before this series is over."

Well, the way he goes after the job was original, anyway. Rube'd had one of his good days the day before and we'd got a trimmin'; but this second day the score was tied up at two runs apiece in the tenth, and Big Jeff'd been wabblin' for two or three innin's.

Well, he walks Saier and me, with one out, and Mac sends for Matty, who was warmed up and ready. John sticks Elliott in in Brid's place and the bug pulls one into the right-field stand.

It's a cinch McGraw thinks well of him then, and might of went after him if he hadn't went crazy the next afternoon. We're tied up in the ninth and Matty's workin'. John sends Elliott up with the bases choked; but he doesn't go right up to the plate. He walks over to their bench and calls McGraw out. Mac tells us about it afterward.

"I can bust up this game right here!" says Elliott.

"Go ahead," says Mac; "but be careful he don't whiff you."

Then the bug pulls it.

"If I whiff," he says, "will you get me on your club?"

"Sure!" says Mac, just as anybody would.

By this time Bill Koem was hollerin' about the delay; so up goes Elliott and gives the worst burlesque on tryin' to hit that you ever see. Matty throws one a mile outside and high, and the bug swings like it was right over the heart. Then Matty throws one at him and he ducks out o' the way—but swings just the same. Matty must of been wise by this time, for he pitches one so far outside that the Chief almost has to go to the coacher's box after it. Elliott takes his third healthy and runs through the field down to the clubhouse.

We got beat in the eleventh; and when we went in to dress he has his street clothes on. Soon as he seen John comin' he says: "I got to see McGraw!" And he beat it.

John was goin' to the fights that night; but before he leaves the hotel he had waivers on Elliott from everybody and had sold him to Atlanta.

"And," says John, "I don't care if they pay for him or not."

My roomy blows in about nine and got the letter from John out of his box. He was goin' to tear it up, but I told him they was news in it. He opens it and reads where he's sold. I was still sore at him; so I says: "Thought you was goin' to get on the New York club?"

"No," he says. "I got turned down cold. McGraw says he wouldn't have me in his club. He says he'd had Charlie Faust—and that was enough for him."

He had a kind o' crazy look in his eyes; so when he starts up to the room I follows him.

"What are you goin' to do now?" I says.

"I'm goin' to sell this ticket to Atlanta," he says, "and go back to Muskegon, where I belong."

"I'll help you pack," I says.

"No," says the bug. "I come into this league with this suit o' clothes and a collar. They can have the rest of it." Then he sits down on the bed and begins to cry like a baby. "No series dough for me," he blubbers, "and no weddin' bells! My girl'll die when she hears about it!"

Of course that made me feel kind o' rotten, and I says:

"Brace up, boy! The best thing you can do is go to Atlanta and try hard. You'll be up here again next year."

"You can't tell me where to go!" he says, and he wasn't cryin' no more. "I'll go where I please—and I'm li'ble to take you with me."

I didn't want no argument, so I kep' still. Pretty soon he goes up to the lookin' glass and stares at himself for five minutes. Then, all of a sudden, he hauls off and takes a wallop at his reflection in the glass. Naturally he smashed the glass all to pieces and he cut his hand somethin' awful.

Without lookin' at it he came over to me and says: "Well, good-by, sport!"—and holds out his other hand to shake. When I starts to shake hands with him he smears his bloody hand all over my map. Then he laughed like a wild man and run out o' the room and out o' the hotel.

VIII

Well, boys, my sleep was broke up for the rest o' the season. It might of been because I was used to sleepin' in all kinds o' racket and excitement, and couldn't stand for the quiet after he'd went—or it might of been because I kep' thinkin' about him and feelin' sorry for him.

I of'en wondered if he'd settle down and be somethin' if he could get married; and finally I got to b'lievin' he would. So when we was dividin' the city series dough I was thinkin' of him and the girl. Our share o' the money—the losers', as usual—was twelve thousand seven hundred sixty bucks or somethin' like that. They was twenty-one of us and that meant six hundred seven bucks apiece. We was just goin' to cut it up that way when I says:

"Why not give a divvy to poor old Elliott?"

About fifteen of 'em at once told me that I was crazy. You see, when he got canned he owed everybody in the club. I guess he'd stuck me for the most about seventy bucks—but I didn't care nothin' about that. I knowed he hadn't never reported to Atlanta, and I thought he was prob'ly busted and a bunch o' money might make things all right for him and the other songbird.

I made quite a speech to the fellers, tellin' 'em how he'd cried when he left us and how his heart'd been set on gettin' married on the series dough. I made it so strong that they finally fell for it. Our shares was cut to five hundred eighty apiece, and John sent him a check for a full share.

For a while I was kind o' worried about what I'd did. I didn't know if I was doin' right by the girl to give him the chance to marry her.

He'd told me she was stuck on him, and that's the only excuse I had for tryin' to fix it up between 'em; but, b'lieve me, if she was my sister or a friend o' mine I'd just as soon of had her manage the Cincinnati Club as marry that bird. I thought to myself:

"If she's all right she'll take acid in a month—and it'll be my fault, but if she's really stuck on him they must be somethin' wrong with her too, so what's the diff'rence?"

Then along comes this letter that I told you about. It's from some friend of his up there—and they's a note from him. I'll read 'em to you and then I got to beat it for the station:

Dear Sir:

They have got poor Elliott locked up and they are goin' to take him to the asylum at Kalamazoo. He thanks you for the check, and we will use the money to see that he is made comf'table.

When the poor boy came back here he found that his girl was married to Joe Bishop, who runs a soda fountain.

She had wrote to him about it, but he did not read her letters. The news drove him crazy—poor boy—and he went to the place where they was livin' with a baseball bat and very near killed 'em both. Then he marched down the street singin' 'Silver Threads

Among the Gold' at the top of his voice. They was gain' to send him to prison for assault with intent to kill, but the jury decided he was crazy.

He wants to thank you again for the money.

Yours truly, Jim—

I can't make out his last name—but it don't make no diff'rence. Now I'll read you his note:

Old Roomy:

I was at bat twice and made two hits; but I guess I did not meet 'em square. They tell me they are both alive yet, which I did not mean 'em to be. I hope they got good curve-ball pitchers where I am gain'. I sure can bust them curves—can't I, sport?

Yours,

B. Elliott.

P.S.—The B stands for Buster.

That's all of it, fellers; and you can see I had some excuse for not hittin'. You can also see why I ain't never goin' to room with no bug again—not for John or nobody else!

THE LONGEST GAME

RALPH D. BLANPIED

The Robins and the Braves celebrated May Day in this ordinarily peaceful city by staging a prolonged, heartbreaking struggle for twenty-six innings at Braves Field and bombing to bits all major-league records for duration of hostilities. When darkness drew its mantle over the scene, both teams were still on their feet, interlocked in a death clutch and each praying for just one more inning in which to get in the knockout blow.

As far as results in the chase for the pennant go the game was without effect, for the final score was 1 to 1.

In the matter of thrills, however, the oldest living man can remember nothing like it, nor can he find anything in his granddad's diary worthy of comparison. Heart disease was the mildest complaint that grasped the spectators as they watched inning after inning slip away and the row of ciphers on the scoreboard began to slide over the fence and reach out into the Fenway.

Nervous prostration threatened to engulf the stands as the twentieth inning passed away in the scoreless routine and word went out from the knowing fans to those of inferior baseball erudition that the National League record was twenty-two innings, the Robins having beaten the Pirates by 6 to 5 in a game of that length played in Brooklyn on Aug. 22, 1917.

The twenty-second inning passed in the history making clash, and then the twenty-third, with a total result of four more ciphers on the scoreboard and a new National League record.

Now the old-timers in the stands began to whisper that the big-league record was twenty-four innings, established in an American League game in the Hub on Sept. 1, 1906, on which occasion the Athletics downed the Red Sox by 4 to 1. The Robins and the Braves didn't care. They didn't even know it. They simply went along in their sublime ignorance and tied this record, then smashed it, and by way of emphasis tacked on a twenty-sixth session.

At this stage of the proceedings Umpire McCormick yawned twice and observed that it was nearly bedtime. He remembered that he had an appointment with a succulent beefsteak and became convinced that it was too dark to play ball. Thereupon he called the game.

The fielding on both sides was brilliant in the crises. Olson saved Brooklyn in the ninth, when, with the bases filled and one out, he stopped Pick's grounder, tagged Powell on the base line and then threw out the batter.

In the seventeenth inning one of the most remarkable double plays ever seen in Boston retired Brooklyn. The bases were filled and one was out when Elliott grounded to Oeschger. Wheat was forced at the plate, but Gowdy's throw to Holke was low and was fumbled. Konetchy tried to score from second and Gowdy received Holke's throw to one side and threw himself blindly across the plate to meet Konetchy's spikes with bare fist.

Joe Oeschger and Leon Cadore were the real outstanding heroes among a score of heroes in the monumental affray of this afternoon.

The two twirlers went the entire distance, each pitching practically the equivalent of three full games in this one contest, and, *mirabile dictu,* instead of showing any sign of weakening under the prolonged strain, each of them appeared to grow stronger. In the final six innings neither artist allowed even the shadow of a safe bingle.

The Braves' twirler had rather the better of the duel in some respects. Fewer hits were made from his delivery than from that of Cadore. Oeschger practically twirled three 3-hit games in a row, while Cadore pitched three 5-hit games in the afternoon's warfare. In only one inning, the seventeenth, did Oeschger allow two safe blows, and Cadore let the local batters group their hits only in the sixth and ninth.

At the receiving end of the batteries, O'Neil gave way to Gowdy for the Braves before hostilities were concluded, and Elliott took Krueger's place behind the bat for Brooklyn.

Robbie's men got their tally in the fifth inning. Krueger was walked by Oeschger, who offended in this way very seldom this afternoon. Krueger went to second while Oeschger was fielding Cadore's little pat and getting his man at first. Ivy Olson slashed a line drive over Maranville's head for a single, on which Krueger crossed home plate. Olson went to second on a wild pitch but was left there as Oeschger tightened up and fanned Neis and Johnston lined to Mann in left field.

The Braves tied the score in the succeeding inning, jamming over the final run of a game which was destined to go on for twenty scoreless innings thereafter, equaling the existing record in this respect. Cadore threw Mann out at first. Cruise came along with a mighty drive to the scoreboard for three bases. Holke popped up a short fly to left which Wheat caught. Boeckel delivered the goods with a single to center upon which Cruise tallied. Maranville followed with a double to center but Boeckel was caught at the plate in the effort to score on the Rabbit's blow, Hood, Cadore and Krueger participating in the put-out.

After this session, save for the Braves' flash in the ninth and the Robins' effort in the seventeenth, the two twirlers were entire masters of the situation.

FULLERTON SAYS SEVEN MEMBERS OF THE WHITE SOX WILL BE MISSING NEXT SPRING

HUGH S. FULLERTON

Cincinnati's Reds are champions of the world. The Reds turned yesterday and gave the dope the worst upsetting it has had during all this surprising and upsetting series. They slashed away at Claude Williams' pitching and before the big crowd had settled to see the contest, it was over. The knockout punch was landed by Duncan, the kid who is the hero of the series and Williams was driven to his retreat and elected to the office of false alarm of the series.

The close of the series was discouraging. Wednesday the dopesters all agreed that the Reds were on the run. The Cincinnati fans who have been canonizing a lot of mediocre athletes turned upon them and declared that they were dogs, yellow curs and German quitters. Yesterday these same Reds swarmed upon the cocky White Sox and battered them into the most humiliating defeat of any world's series.

There will be a great deal written and talked about this world's series. There will be a lot of inside stuff that never will be printed, but the truth will remain that the team which was the hardest working, which fought hardest, and which stuck together to the end won. The team which excelled in mechanical skill, which had the ability, individually, to win, was beaten.

EVERYTHING GOES BACKWARD

They spilled the dope terribly. Almost everything went backward, so much so that an evil minded person might believe the stories that have been circulated during the series. The fact is that this series was lost in the first game, and lost through over confidence. Forget the suspicious and evil minded yarns that may be circulated. The Reds are not the better club. They are not even the best club in their own league, but they play ball together, fight together and hustle together, and remember that a flivver that keeps running beats a Roll Royce that is missing on several cylinders. The Sox were missing on several.

They played the game as a team only through one game, and part of another, and they deserved defeat. It is not up to me to decide why they did such things. That all probably will come out in the wash. They were licked and licked good and proper, deserved it, and got it.

Yesterday's game in all probability is the last that ever will be played in any world's series. If the club owners and those who have the interests of the game at heart have listened during this series they will call off the annual inter-league contests. If they value the good name of the sport they will do so beyond doubt.

Yesterday's game also means the disruption of the Chicago White Sox as a ball club. There are seven men on the team who will not be there when the gong sounds next Spring and some of them will not be in either major league.

HIS OWN STUFF

CHARLES E. VAN LOAN

It's a mighty fine thing for a man to know when he's had enough, but there's a piece of knowledge which beats it all hollow.

That's for him to know when his friends have had too much.

This is no temperance sermon, so you needn't quit reading. It's the story of a baseball player who thought he was funny and didn't know when to quit the rough-and-tumble comedy that some idiot has named practical joking.

Before I tell you what happened to Tom O'Connor because he didn't know when to quit being funny, I want to put myself on record. I don't believe that there is any such a thing as a practical joke. As I understand the word, a thing in order to be practical must have some sense to it and be of some use to people. To play it safe I looked up the dictionary definition of the word to see if I could stretch it far enough to cover the sort of stuff that Tom O'Connor pulled on us at the training camp last season. I couldn't make it answer. Here's what I found in the dictionary:

> "PRACTICAL—pertaining to or governed by actual use or experience, as contrasted with ideals, speculations and theories."

That's what the big book says it means, and I string with the definition whether I understand all of it or not. Show me anything in there that applies to sawing out half the slats in a man's bed or mixing up all the shoes in a Pullman car at three o'clock in the morning!

You can call it practical joking if you want to, but it won't go with me. I claim there's nothing practical about it, or sensible either. Practical joking is just another name for plain, ordinary foolishness with a mean streak in it. The main thing about a practical joke is that somebody always gets hurt—usually an innocent party.

I'm strong for a good clever joke. I get as much fun out of one as anybody and I can laugh when the joke is on me; but when it comes to the rough stuff I pass. Take 'em as a whole, baseball players are a jolly bunch. They've got youth and health and vitality. They call us the Old Guard, but we're really nothing but a lot of young fellows and we have the reputation of being the liveliest outfit in the league; but even so, we got sick of the sort of stunts that Tom O'Connor handed us at the training camp and in the early part of the season.

We didn't have much of a line on Tom when he joined the club. He'd been in the big league only part of the season previously, and he came to the Old Guard as the result of a winter trade. We needed a first-baseman the worst way, and Uncle Billy—he's our manager— gave up a pitcher, an infielder and an outfielder to get Tom O'Connor away from the Blues. The newspapers made an awful roar about that trade, and so did the fans. They said Uncle Billy was out of his head and was trying to wreck the team by letting three good men go. The noise they made wasn't a whisper to the howl that went up from the other manager when the time came to get some work out of those three good men.

When it comes to a swap, Uncle Billy is a tougher proposition than a Connecticut Yank, and a Connecticut Yank can take an Armenian pawnbroker's false teeth away from him and give him Brazil nuts in exchange for 'em. Uncle Billy always hands the other managers three or four men for one. He's so liberal and open-hearted that they feel sorry for him, and they keep right on feeling sorry after they see what he's slipped them in the trade.

In this case the pitcher had a strained ligament that even the bone-setter couldn't fix, the infielder's eyes were giving out on him and the outfielder had a permanent charley-horse in his left leg. As big-league ballplayers they were all through, but as benchwarmers and salary grabbers they were immense.

Even if they had been in condition I think that Tom O'Connor would have been worth the three, for he is a cracking good first-base-man, and now that he has settled down to business and quit being the team comedian he'll be even better than he was last year.

He joined us at the spring training camp in Louisiana. We've been going to the same place for years. It's a sort of health resort with rotten water to drink and baths; and the hotel is always full of broken-down old men with whiskers and fat wives to look after 'em.

O'Connor turned up in the mam dining-room the first night with a big box of marshmallows in his hand. He is a tall, handsome chap with a tremendous head of hair and a smile that sort of warms you to him even after you know him. He stopped at every table and invited folks to help themselves.

"These are very choice, madam; something new in confectionery. Prepared by a friend of mine. Won't you try one?"

That was his spiel, but the smile and the little twinkle of the eye that went with it was what did the business. The fat ladies didn't stop to think that it was rather unusual for a strange young man to be offer-ing them candy. They smiled back at Tom and helped themselves to the marshmallows, and some of them insisted that their husbands should try one too. Tom was a smooth, rapid worker and he kept moving, not stopping long at a table and never looking back. Perhaps that was just as well, for the marshmallow had been dipped in powdered quinine instead of powdered sugar. Quinine ain't so bad when you expect it, but when your mouth is all fixed for marshmallow the disappointment and the quinine together make a strong combination. The fat ladies went out of the dining-room on the run, choking into their handkerchiefs, and the old men sent C. Q. D.s for the proprietor. He came in and Tom met him at the door and handed him one of the marshmallows, and then of course everybody laughed.

I admit that we might have begun discouraging his comedy right there. We would have done it if he'd been a minor-leaguer trying to break in, but he wasn't. He'd been five months with the Blues—a bad ball club, but still in the big league. That made him one of us. We knew and he knew that he was going to be our first-baseman and he settled down with as much assurance as if he had been with us ten years instead of ten hours.

He saw right away that we were going to be a good audience for him. Not all of his stuff was on the rough-house order. Some of us were not long in finding that out.

A couple of nights afterward we were having a nice, quiet little game of draw poker in my room on the third floor of the hotel. Any poker game running after ten o'clock in the same hotel with Uncle Billy has got to be a quiet one—or it's a case of a fifty-dollar fine all round.

Uncle Billy is a great baseball manager but he's awfully narrow-gauge on certain subjects, and one of 'em is the American indoor national pastime of draw poker. He doesn't like the game for seven hundred different reasons, but mainly because he says it sets a bad example to the kid players, who get to gambling among themselves and lose more than they can afford. That's true of course, but if a kid is born with the gambling bug in his system you can't fine it out of him, not even at fifty a smash. One season Uncle Billy tried to shut down on poker altogether, and there was more poker played that year than ever before. Then he took off the lid, and now we're allowed to play twenty-five-cent limit until ten o'clock at night. Think of it! Why, if a man had all the luck in the world and filled everything he drew to he might win as much as four dollars!

I'm not saying that the rule isn't a good one for recruits and kids, but it comes hard on the veterans, especially at the training camp where there isn't a thing to do after dark. We used to sneak a real game once in a while with a blanket over the transom and paper stuffed in the cracks and the keyhole. We had to do that because we couldn't trust Uncle Billy. He was just underhanded enough to listen outside of door, and to make it worse the poor old coot has insomnia and we never know when he's asleep and when he's not.

Well, this poker party in my room was the real thing: Pat Dunphy, Holliday, Satterfield, Meadows, Daly and myself—all deep-sea pirates. It was table-stakes of course, every man declaring fifty or a hundred behind his stack in case he should pick up something heavy and want action on it.

It got to be about two in the morning, and Dunphy was yawning his head off and looking at his watch every few minutes. He was two hundred ahead. The rest of us were up and down, seesawing along and waiting for a set of fours or something. The elevators had quit running long ago and there wasn't a sound in the hotel anywhere. What talking we did was in whispers because we never knew when Uncle Billy might take it into his head to go for a walk. I've known him to bust up a poker game at four in the morning.

Dunphy was just scooping in another nice pot—like a fool I played my pat straight against his onecard draw—when all of a sudden a board creaked in the hall outside, and then came a dry, raspy little cough that we knew mighty well.

"Holy Moses!" whispered Dunphy. "Uncle Billy! Don't move!"

Then somebody pounded on the door. We were sure there wasn't any light showing through the cracks, so we sat quiet a few seconds trying to think what to do. The pounding began again, louder than before—bangety bang-bang!

Well, our only chance was to keep Uncle Billy out of the room, so I motioned to the boys and they picked up their money and chips and tiptoed into the alcove in the corner. I whipped off my shirt, kicked off my pants, put on a bathrobe, tousled up my hair to make it look as if I'd been asleep a week, switched out the light and opened the door a few inches. Then I stepped out into the hall.

It was empty from end to end. There wasn't a soul in sight.

We had a long discussion about it. We all agreed that it was Uncle Billy's cough we heard; but why had he hammered on the door so hard and then gone away? That wasn't like him. Had he been round to the other rooms checking up on us? Was he so sure of us that he didn't need the actual evidence? Perhaps he was going to switch his system and begin fining people fifty dollars apiece on circumstantial evidence. It began to have all the earmarks of an expensive evening for the six of us.

"Did anybody else know about this party?" I asked.

"O'Connor knew," Holliday spoke up. "I asked him if he didn't want to play a little poker. He said he couldn't take a chance of getting in Dutch with the boss so soon. That was his excuse, but maybe he was a little light in the vest pocket. He already knew about the ten o'clock rule and the fifty-dollar fine."

"Did he know we were going to play in this room?"

"Sure, but I don't see where you figure him. He wouldn't have tipped it off to anybody. Probably Uncle Billy couldn't sleep and was prowling round. You can't get away from that cough. And he's got us dead to rights or he wouldn't have gone away. I'll bet he's had a pass-key and been in every one of our rooms. We'll hear from him in the morning."

It did look that way. We settled up and the boys slipped out one at a time, carrying their shoes in their hands. I don't know about the rest of 'em, but I didn't sleep much. The fifty-dollar fine didn't bother me, but Uncle Billy has got a way of throwing in a roast along with it.

I dreaded to go down to breakfast in the morning. Uncle Billy usually has a table with his wife and kids close to the door, so he can give us the once-over as we come in.

"Morning, Bob!" says Uncle Billy, smiling over his hotcakes. "How do you feel this morning?"

"Finer'n split silk!" says I, and went on over to the main. table with the gang. That started me to wondering, because if Uncle Billy had anything on me he wouldn't have smiled. The best I could have expected was a black look and a grunt. Uncle Billy was a poor hand at hiding his feelings. If he was peeved with you it showed in everything he did. I didn't know what to make of that smile, and that's what had me worried.

Dunphy and Holliday and the others were puzzled too, and the suspense was eating us up. We sat there, looking silly and fooling with our knives and forks, every little while stealing a peek at each other. We couldn't figure it at all. Tom O'Connor was at one end of the table eating like a longshoreman and saying nothing. Dunphy stood the strain as 'long as he could and then he cracked.

"Did Uncle Billy call on any of you fellows last night?" said he.

"No! Was he sleep-walking again, the old rascal?"

"Was anything doing?"

"He never came near the fourth floor. If he had he'd 'a' busted up a hot little crap game."

"What was he looking for—poker?"

None of the boys had seen him. It was plain that if Uncle Billy had been night-prowling we were the only ones that he had bothered. Peachy Parsons spoke up.

"Did you see him, Pat?" says he.

"Why, no," says Dunphy. "I—I heard him."

For a few seconds there was dead silence. Then Tom O'Connor shoved his chair back, stood up, looked all round the table with a queer grin on his face and coughed once—that same dry, raspy little cough. It sounded so much like Uncle Billy that we all jumped.

O'Connor didn't wait for the laugh. He walked out of the dining-room and left us looking at each other with our mouths open.

II

I knew a busher once who tore off a home run the first time he came to bat in the big league, and it would have been a lot better for him if he had struck out. The fans got to calling him Home-Run Slattery and he got to thinking he was all of that. He wouldn't have a base on balls as a gift and he wouldn't bunt. He wanted to knock the cover off every ball he saw. Uncle Billy shipped him back to Texas in June, and he's there yet. In a way O'Connor reminded me of that busher.

He had made a great start as a comedian. The stuff that he put over on the poker players was clever and legitimate; there was real fun in it. His reputation as a two-handed kidder was established then and there, and he might have rested on it until he thought of something else as good. He might have; but we laughed at him, and then of course he wanted to put the next one over the fence too.

I can see now looking back at it, that we were partly responsible. You know how it is with a comedian—the more you laugh at him, the worse he gets. Pretty soon he wants laughs all the time, and if they're not written into his part he tries to make 'em up as he goes along. If he hasn't got any new, clever ideas he pulls old stuff or rough stuff-in other words he gets to be a slapstick comedian. A good hiss or two or a few rotten eggs at the right time would teach him to stay with legitimate work.

It didn't take Tom long to run out of clever comedy and get down to the rough stuff. Rough stuff is the backbone of practical joking. Things began to happen round the training camp. We couldn't actually prove 'em on Tom at the time—and we haven't proved 'em on him yet—but the circumstantial evidence is all against him. He wouldn't have a chance with a jury of his peers—whatever they are.

Tom began easy and worked up his speed by degrees. His first stunts were mild ones, such as leaving a lot of bogus calls with the night clerk and getting a lot of people rung out of bed at four in the morning; but of course that wasn't funny enough to suit him.

There was a girl from Memphis stopping at the hotel, and Joe Holliday the pitcher thought pretty well of her. He borrowed an automobile one Sunday to take her for a ride. After they were about twenty miles from town the engine sneezed a few times and laid down cold.

"Don't worry," says Holliday, "I know all about automobiles. I'll have this bird flying again in a minute."

"It sounded to me as if you'd run out of gas," said the girl, who knew something about cars herself.

"Impossible!" says Holliday. "I had the tank filled this morning and you can see there's no leak."

"Well, I don't know all about automobiles," says the girl, "but you'd better take a look in that tank."

That made Holliday a little sore, because he'd bought twenty gallons of gasoline and paid for it. They stayed there all day and Holliday messed round in the bowels of the beast and got full of oil and grease and dirt. I'll bet he stored up enough profanity inside of him to last for the rest of his natural life. And all the time the girl kept fussing about the gasoline tank. Finally, after Joe had done everything else that he could think of, he unscrewed the cap and the gas tank was dry as a bone.

Somebody with a rare sense of humour had drawn off about seventeen gallons of gasoline.

"I told you so!" said the girl—which is just about what a girl would say under the circumstances.

They got back to the hotel late that night. Love's young dream had run out with the gasoline, and from what I could gather they must have quarrelled all the way home. Joe went down and got into a fight with the man at the garage and was hit over the head with a monkey-wrench. From now on you'll notice that Tom's comedy was mostly physical and people were getting hurt every time.

Joe's troubles lasted O'Connor for a couple of days and then he hired a darky boy to get him a water snake. I think he wrote it in the boy's contract that the snake had to be harmless or there was nothing doing. He put the snake, a whopping big striped one, between the sheets in Al Jorgenson's bed, which is my notion of no place in the world to put a snake. Jorgenson is our club secretary—a middle-aged fellow who never has much to say and attends strictly to business.

Al rolled on to the snake in the dark, but it seems he knew what it was right away. He wrecked half the furniture, tore the door off the hinges and came fluttering down into the lobby, yelling murder at every jump. It was just his luck that the old ladies were all present. They were pulling off a whist tournament that night, but they don't know yet who won. Al practically spoiled the whole evening for 'em.

The charitable way to look at it is that Tom didn't know that Jorgenson was hitting the booze pretty hard and kept a quart bottle in his room. If he had known that, maybe he would have wished the snake on to a teetotaler, like Uncle Billy. To make it a little more abundant Tom slipped in and copped the snake while Al was doing his shirt-tail specialty, and when we got him back to the room there wasn't any snake there. Tom circulated round among the old ladies and told 'em not to be alarmed in the least because maybe it wasn't a real snake that Jorgenson saw.

But Tom had his good points after all. The next morning Al found the snake tied to his door-knob, which relieved his mind a whole lot; but he was so mortified and ashamed that he had all his meals in his room after that and used to come and go by the kitchen entrance.

Tom's next stunt—which he didn't make any secret of—put four of the kid recruits out of business. He framed up a midnight hunt for killyloo birds. It's the old snipe trick. I didn't believe that there were four people left in the world who would fall for that stunt. It was invented by one of old man Pharaoh's boys in the days of the Nile Valley League. It is hard to find one man in the whole town who will fall for it, because it has been so well advertised, but Tom grabbed four in a bunch. It just goes to show how much solid ivory a baseball scout can dig up when his travelling expenses are paid.

The idea is very simple. First you catch a sucker and take him out in the woods at night. You give him a sack and a candle. He's to keep the candle lighted and hold the mouth of the sack open so that you can drive the killyloo birds into it. The main point is to make it perfectly clear to the sucker that a killyloo bird when waked out of a sound sleep always walks straight to the nearest light to get his feet warm. After the sucker understands that thoroughly you can leave him and go home to bed. He sits there with his candle, fighting mosquitoes and wondering what has become of you and why the killyloo birds don't show up.

Tom staged his production in fine style. He rented a livery rig and drove those poor kids eleven miles into a swamp. If you have ever seen a Louisiana swamp you can begin laughing now. He got 'em planted so far apart that they couldn't do much talking, explained all about the peculiar habits of the sleepy killyloos, saw that their candles were burning nicely and then went away to herd in the game. He was back at the hotel by eleven o'clock.

About midnight the boys held a conference and decided that maybe it was a bad time of the year for killyloo birds but that the sucker crop hadn't been cut down any. They started back for the hotel on foot and got lost in mud clear up to their necks. They stayed in the swamp all night and it's a wonder that they got out alive. And that wasn't all: Uncle Billy listened to their tales of woe and said if they didn't have any more sense than that they wouldn't make ballplayers, so he sent 'em home.

The night before we were to leave for the North there was a little informal dance at the hotel and the town folks came in to meet the ballplayers and learn the tango and the hesitation waltz.

It was a perfectly bully party and everything went along fine until the punch was brought in. We'd decided not to have any liquor in it on account of the strong prohibition sentiment in the community, so we had a kind of a fruit lemonade with grape juice in it.

Well, those fat old ladies crowded round the bowl as if they were perishing of thirst. They took one swig of the punch and went sailing for the elevators like full-rigged ships in a gale of wind.

Of course I thought I knew what was wrong. It's always considered quite a joke to slip something into the punch. I'd been dancing with a swell little girl and as we started for the punch-bowl I said:

"You won't mind if this punch has got a wee bit of a kick in it, will you?"

"Not in the least," said she. "Father always puts a little brandy in ours."

So that was all right and I ladled her out a sample. I would have got mine at the same time, but an old lady behind me started to choke and I turned round to see what was the matter. When I turned back to the girl again there were tears in her eyes and she was sputtering about rowdy ballplayers. She said that she had a brother at college who could lick all the big-leaguers in the world, and she hoped he'd begin on me. Then she went out of the room with her nose in the air.

I was terribly upset about it because I couldn't think what I had done that was wrong, and just because I had the glass in my hand I began drinking the punch. Then I went out and climbed a telegraph pole and yelled for the fire department. Talk about going crazy with the heat. It can be done, believe me! I felt like a general-alarm fire for the rest of the evening.

There was an awful fuss about that, and some of us held a council of war. We decided to put it up to O'Connor. He stood pat in a very dignified way and said that he must positively refuse to take the blame for anything unless there was proof that he did it. About that time the cook found two empty tabasco sauce bottles under the kitchen sink. That didn't prove anything. We already knew what the stuff was and that too much of it had been used. One bottle would have been a great plenty.

That was the situation when we started North. Everybody felt that it was dangerous to be safe with a physical humourist like

O'Connor on the payroll. We hoped that he'd quit playing horse and begin to play ball.

We went so far as to hint that the next rough stuff he put over on the bunch would bring him before the Kangaroo Court and it wouldn't make any difference whether we had any evidence or not. The Kangaroo Court is the last word in physical humour. It's even rougher than taking the Imperial Callithumpian Degree in the Order of the Ornery and Worthless Men of the World.

The last straw fell on us in the home town. Jorgenson came into the dressing room one afternoon with a handful of big square envelopes. There was one for every man on the team.

I opened mine and there was a stiff sheet of cardboard inside of it printed in script. I didn't save mine, but it read something like this:

Mr. Augustus P. Stringer requests the honour of your company at dinner, at the Algonquin Club, 643 — Avenue, at seven-thirty on the evening of May the Twelfth, Nineteen Hundred and —. Formal.

Well, there was quite a buzz of excitement over it. "Who is this Mr. Stringer?" asks Uncle Billy.

"Any of you boys know him?"

Nobody seemed to, but that wasn't remarkable. All sorts of people give dinners to ballplayers during the playing season. I've seen some winters when a good feed would come in handy, but a ballplayer is only strong with the public between April and October. The rest of the year nobody cares very much whether he eats or not.

"He's probably some young sport who wants to show us a good time and brag about what a whale of a ballplayer he used to be in college," says Pat Dunphy.

"You're wrong!" says Peachy Parsons. "Ten to one you're wrong! I never saw this Mr. Stringer, but I'll bet I've got him pegged to a whisper. In the first place I know about this Algonquin Club. It's the oldest and the most exclusive club in the city. Nothing but rich men belong to it. You can go by there any night and see 'em sitting in the windows, holding their stomachs in their laps. Now this Mr. Stringer is probably a nice old man with a sneaking liking for baseball. He wants to entertain us, but at the same time he's afraid that we're a lot of lowbrows and that we'll show him up before the other club members."

"What makes you think that?" asks Dunphy. "Simple enough. He's got an idea that we don't know what to wear to a banquet, so he tips us off. He puts 'formal' down in one corner."

"What does that mean?"

"It's not usually put on an invitation. It means the old thirteen-and-the-odd. Clawhammer, white tie, silk hat and all the rest of it."

"How about a 'tux'?"

"Absolutely barred. A tuxedo isn't formal."

"That settles it!" says Dunphy "I don't go. If this bird don't want to see me in my street clothes he don't need to see me at all. I never bought one of those beetle-backed coats and I never will!"

"Come now," says Uncle Billy, "don't get excited. I know a place where you can rent an entire outfit for two bucks, shoes and all."

"Oh, well," says Dunphy, "in that case—"

The more we talked about it, the stronger we were taken with the idea. It would be something to say that we'd had dinner at the Algonquin Club. We warned Tom O'Connor that none of his rough comedy would go. He got awfully sore about it. One word led to another and finally he said if we felt that way about it he wouldn't go. We tried to persuade him that it wasn't quite the thing to turn down an invitation, but he wouldn't listen.

You never saw such a hustling round or such a run on the gents' furnishing goods. Everybody was buying white shirts, white ties and silk socks. If we were going to do it at all we felt that it might as well be done right, and of course we wanted to show Mr. Stringer that we knew what was what. Those who didn't own evening clothes hired 'em for the occasion, accordion hats and all. We met a couple of blocks away from the club and marched over in a body like a lot of honourary pall-bearers.

We got by the outer door all right and into the main room where some old gentlemen were sitting round, smoking cigars and reading the newspapers. They seemed kind of annoyed about something and looked at us as if they took us for burglars in disguise, which they probably did. Up comes a flunky in uniform, knee-breeches and mutton-chop whiskers. Uncle Billy did the talking for the bunch.

"Tell Mr. Stringer that we're here," says he. "I—beg your pardon?" says the flunky.

"You don't need to do that," says" Uncle Billy. "Just run along and tell Mr. Stringer that his guests are here."

The flunky seemed puzzled for a minute, and then he almost smiled.

"Ah!" says he. "The—Democratic Club is on the opposite corner, sir. Possibly there has been some mistake."

Uncle Billy began to get sore. He flashed his invitation and waved it under the flunky's nose.

"It says here the Algonquin Club. You don't look it, but maybe you can read."

"Oh, yes, sir," says the flunky. He examined the invitation carefully and then he shook his head. "Very, very sorry, sir," says he, "but there is some mistake."

"How can there be any mistake?" roars Uncle Billy. "Where is Mr. Stringer?"

"That is what I do not know, sir," says the flunky. "We have no such member, sir."

Well, that was a knock-out. Even Uncle Billy didn't know what to say to that. The rest of us stood round on one foot and then on the other like a lot of clothing-store dummies. One of the old gentlemen motioned to the flunky, who left us, but not without looking back every few seconds as if he expected us to start something.

"James," pipes up the old gentleman, "perhaps they have been drinking. Have you telephoned for the police?"

"They don't seem to be violent yet, sir," says James. Then he came back to us and explained again that he was very, very sorry, but there must be some mistake. No Mr. Stringer was known at the Algonquin Club.

"This way out, gentlemen," says James.

I think I was the first one that tumbled to it. We were going down the steps when it struck me like a thousand of brick.

"Stringer!" says I. "We've been strung all right. Tom O'Connor has gone back to the legitimate!"

"No wonder he didn't want to come!" says everybody at once.

We stood on the corner under the lamppost and held an indignation meeting, the old gentlemen looking down at us from the windows as if they couldn't make up their minds whether we were dangerous or not. We hadn't decided what we ought to do with Tom when the reporters began to arrive. That cinched it. Every paper had been tipped off by telephone that there was a good josh story at the Algonquin Club, and the funny men had been turned loose on it. Uncle Billy grabbed me by the arm.

"Tip the wink to Dunphy and Parsons and let's get out of this," says he. "I don't often dude myself up and it seems a shame to waste it. We will have dinner at the Casino and frame up a come-back on O'Connor."

I've always said that, in spite of his queer notions about certain things, Uncle Billy is a regular human being. The dinner that he bought us that night proved it, and the idea that he got, along with the coffee, made it even stronger.

"Do you boys know any actresses?" said he. "I mean any that are working in town now?"

"I know Hazel Harrington," says Parsons.

"Ah-hah," says Uncle Billy. "That's the pretty one in Paris Up to Date, eh?" Why, the old rascal even had a line on the musical comedy stars! "Is she a good fellow?"

"Best in the world!" says Parsons. "And a strong baseball fan."

"Fine!" says Uncle Billy and he snapped his fingers at a waiter. "Pencil and paper and messenger boy—quick! Now then, Peachy, write this lady a note and say that we will be highly honoured if she will join us here after the show to discuss a matter of grave importance to the Old Guard. Say that you will call in a taxi to get her."

When the note had gone Uncle Billy lighted a fresh cigar and chuckled to himself.

"If she'll go through with it," says he, "I'll guarantee to knock all the funny business out of Tom O'Connor for the rest of his natural life."

Miss Harrington turned up about eleven-thirty, even prettier off the stage than on it, which is going some. She said that she had side-stepped a date with a Pittsburgh millionaire because we were real people. That was a promising start. She ordered a light supper of creamed lobster and champagne and then Uncle Billy began to talk.

He told her that as a manager he was in a bad fix. He said he had a new man on the payroll who was promoting civil war. He explained that unless he was able to tame this fellow the team would be crippled. Miss Harrington said that would be a pity, for she had bet on us to win the pennant. She wanted to know what was the matter. Uncle Billy told her all about Tom O'Connor and his practical jokes. Miss Harrington said it would be a good thing to give him a dose of his own medicine. It was like Uncle Billy to let her think that the idea belonged to her.

"Suppose," says Uncle Billy, "you should get a note from him, asking you to meet him at the stage door some night next week. For the sake of the ball club, would you say 'Yes'?"

"But—what would happen after that?" asked Miss Harrington. "I don't know the man at all and—"

Uncle Billy told her what would happen after that, and as it dawned on the rest of us we nearly rolled out of our chairs. Miss Harrington laughed too.

"It would be terribly funny," said she, "and I suppose it would serve him right; but it might get into the papers and—"

Uncle Billy shook his head.

"My dear young lady," says he, "the only publicity that you get in this town is the publicity that you go after. I am well and favourably known to the police. A lot of 'em get annual passes from me. Captain Murray at the Montmorency Street Station is my pal. He can see a joke without plans and specifications. I promise you that the whole thing will go off like clockwork. We'll suppose that you have attracted the young man's attention during the performance. You would attract any man's attention, my dear."

"I would stand up and bow for that compliment," said Miss Harrington, "but the waiter is looking. Go on."

"We will suppose that you have received a note from him," said Uncle Billy. "He is to meet you at the stage door. . . . One tiny little scream—just one. . . . Would you do that—for the sake of the ball club?"

Miss Harrington giggled.

"If you're sure that you can keep me out of it," said she, "I'll do it for the sake of the joke!"

Uncle Billy was a busy man for a few days, but he found time to state that he didn't believe that Tom O'Connor had anything to do with the Algonquin Club thing. He said it was so clever that Tom couldn't have thought of it, and he said it in the dressing room so loud that everybody heard him. Maybe that was the reason why Tom didn't suspect anything when he was asked to fill out a box party.

Pat Dunphy, Peachy Parsons and some of the rest of us were in on the box party, playing thinking parts mostly. Uncle Billy and Tom O'Connor had the front seats right up against the stage.

Miss Harrington was immense. If she'd had forty rehearsals she couldn't have done it any better. Before she'd been on the stage three minutes Tom was fumbling round for his programme trying to find her name. Pretty soon he began to squirm in his chair.

"By golly, that girl is looking at me all the time!" says he.

"Don't kid yourself!" said Uncle Billy.

"But I tell you she is! There—did you see that?"

"Maybe she wants to meet you," says Uncle Billy.

"I've seen her at the ball park a lot of times."

"You think she knows who I am?" asks Tom.

"Shouldn't wonder. You're right, Tom. She's after you, that's a fact."

"Oh, rats!" says O'Connor. "Maybe I just think so. No, there it is again! Do you suppose, if I sent my card back—"

"I'm a married man," says Uncle Billy. "I don't suppose anything. But if a girl as pretty as that—"

Tom went out at the end of the first act. I saw him write something on a card and slip it to an usher along with a dollar bill.

When the second act opened Tom was so nervous he couldn't sit still. It was easy to see that he hadn't received any answer to his note and was worrying about it. Pretty soon Miss Harrington came on to sing her song about the moon—they've always got to have a moon song in musical comedy or it doesn't go—and just as the lights went down she looked over toward our box and smiled, the least little bit of a smile, and then she nodded her head. The breath went out of Tom O'Connor in a long sigh.

"Somebody lend me twenty dollars," says he. "I'm going to meet her at the stage door after the show," says Tom, "and she won't think I'm a sport unless I open wine."

Well, he met her all right enough. The whole bunch of us can swear to that because we were across the street, hiding in a doorway. When she came out Tom stepped up, chipper as a canary bird, with his hat in his hand. We couldn't hear what he said, but there was no trouble in hearing Miss Harrington.

"How dare you, sir!" she screams. "Help! Police! Help!"

Two men, who had been loafing round on the edge of the sidewalk, jumped over and grabbed Tom by the arms. He started in to explain matters to 'em, but the men dragged him away down the street and Miss Harrington went in the other direction.

"So far, so good," says Uncle Billy. "Gentlemen, the rest of the comedy will be played out at the Montmorency Street Police Station. Reserved seats are waiting for us. Follow me."

You can say anything you like, but it's a pretty fine thing to be in right with the police. You never know when you may need 'em, and Uncle Billy certainly was an ace at the Montmorency Street Station. We went in by the side door and were shown into a little narrow room with a lot of chairs in it, just like a moving-picture theatre, except that instead of a curtain at the far end there was a tall Japanese screen. What was more, most of the chairs were occupied. Every member of the Old Guard ball club was there, and so was Al Jorgenson and Lije, the rubber.

"Boys," says Uncle Billy, "we are about to have the last act of the thrilling drama entitled The Kidder Kidded, or The Old Guard's Revenge. The first and second acts went off fine. Be as quiet as you can and don't laugh until the blow-off. Not a whisper—not a sound—s-s-sh! They're bringing him in now!"

There was a scuffling of feet and a scraping of chair-legs on the other side of the screen. We couldn't see O'Connor and he couldn't see us, but we could hear every word he said. He was still trying to explain matters.

"But I tell you," says Tom, "I had a date with her."

"Yeh," says a gruff voice, "she acted like it! Don't tell us your troubles. Tell 'em to Captain Murray. Here he comes now."

A door opened and closed and another voice cut in: "Well, boys, what luck?"

"We got one, cap," says the gruff party. "Caught him with the goods on—"

"It's all a mistake, sir—captain!" Tom breaks in. "I give you my word of honour as a gentleman—"

"Shut up!" says Captain Murray. "Your word of honour as a gentleman! That's rich, that is! You keep your trap closed for the present—understand? Now, boys, where did you get him?"

"At the stage door of the Royal Theatre," says the plain-clothes man, who did the talking for the two who made the pinch. "Duffy and me, we saw this bird kind of slinking round, and we remembered that order about bringing in all mashers, so we watched him. A girl came out of the stage door and he braced her. She hollered for help and we grabbed him. Oh, there ain't any question about it, cap; we've got him dead to rights. We don't even need the woman's testimony."

"Good work, boys!" says the captain. "We'll make an example of this guy!"

"Captain," says Torn, "listen to reason! I tell you this girl was flirting with me all through the show—"

"That's what they all say! If she was flirting with you, why did she make a holler when you braced her?"

"I—I don't know," says Torn. "Maybe she didn't recognise me."

"No, I'll bet she didn't!"

"But, captain, I sent her my card and she sent back word—"

"Oh, shut up! What's your name?" Murray shot that one at him quick and Torn took a good long time to answer it.

"Smith," says he at last. "John Smith." That raised a laugh on the other side of the screen.

"Well," says the captain, "unless we can get him identified he can do his bit on the rock pile under the name of Smith as well as any other, eh, boys?"

"Sure thing!" said the plain-clothes men.

"The rock pile!" says Torn.

"That's what I said—rock pile! Kind of scares you, don't it? There won't be any bail for you to jump or any fine for you to pay. We've had a lot of complaints about mashers lately and some squeals in the newspapers. You'll be made an example of. Chickens are protected by the game laws of this state, and it's time some of the lady-killers found it out."

Tom began to plead, but he might just as well have kept quiet. They whirled in and gave him the third degree—asked him what he had been pinched for the last time and a whole lot of stuff. We expected he'd tell his name and send for Uncle Billy to get him out, but for some reason or other he fought shy of that. We couldn't understand his play at first, but we knew why soon enough. The door back of the screen opened again.

"Cap'n," says a strange voice, "there's some newspaper men here."

Well, that was all a stall, of course. We didn't let the newspaper men in on it because we wanted them for a whip to hold over Tom's head in the future.

"What do they want?" asks Murray.

"They're after this masher story," says the stranger. "I don't know who tipped it off to 'em, but they've seen the woman and got a statement from her. She says she thinks this follow is a baseball player."

"I wouldn't care if he was the president of the League!" says the captain. "You know the orders we got to break up mashing and bring 'em in, no matter who they are. Here we've got one of 'em dead to rights; and it's the rock pile for him, you can bet your life on it!"

"And serve him right," says the stranger. "But, cap'n, wouldn't it be a good thing to identify him? These newspapermen say they know all the ballplayers. Shall we have 'em in to give him the once-over?"

"I'll send for 'em in a minute," says Murray.

That was the shot that brought Tom off his perch with a yell.

"Captain," he begs, "anything but that! I'd rather you sent me up for six months—yes, or shot me! If this gets into the papers it'll—! Oh say, if you have any heart at all—please—please—Oh, you don't understand!"

We didn't understand either, but Tom made it plain. I'm not going to write all he said; it made my face burn to sit there and listen to it. It took all the fun out of the joke for me. It seems that this rough kidder—this practical joker who never cared a rap how much he hurt anybody else's feelings—had some pretty tender feelings of his own. He opened up his heart and told that police captain something that he never had told us—told him about the little girl back in the home town who was waiting for him, and how she wouldn't ever be able to hold up her head again if the story got into the papers and he was disgraced.

"It ain't for me, captain," he begs; "it's for her. You wouldn't want her shamed just because I've acted like a fool, would you? Think what it means to the girl, captain! Oh, if there's anything you can do—"

Uncle Billy beat me to it. I was already on my feet when he took two jumps and knocked the screen flat on the floor.

"That's enough!" says Uncle Billy. We had planned to give Tom the horse-laugh when the screen came down, but somehow none of us could laugh just then. If I live to be as old as Hans Wagner I'll never forget the expression on Tom O'Connor's face as he blinked across the room and saw us all sitting there, like an audience in a theatre.

"Tom," says Uncle Billy, "I'm sorry, but this is what always happens with a practical joke. It starts out to be funny, but it gets away from you and then the first thing you know somebody is hurt. You've had a lot of fun with this ball club, my boy, and some of it was pretty rough fun, but—I guess we'll all agree to call it square."

Tom got on his feet, shaking a little and white to the lips. He couldn't seem to find his voice for a minute and he ran his fingers across his mouth before he spoke.

"Is—is this a joke?" says he.

"It started out to be," says Uncle Billy. "I'm sorry."

Tom didn't say another word and he didn't look at any of us. He went out of the room alone and left us there. I wanted to go after him and tell him not to take it so hard; but I thought of the way he had shamed Al Jorgenson, I thought of the girl who wouldn't even speak to Holliday again, I thought of the four kids who went home broken-hearted, all on Tom's account—and I changed my mind. It was a bitter dose, but I decided not to sweeten it any for him.

Tom O'Connor isn't funny any more, and I think he is slowly making up his mind that we're not such a bad outfit after all. To this day the mention of the name of Smith makes him blush, so I guess that in spite of the fact that he's never opened his mouth about it since, he hasn't forgotten what his own stuff feels like.

THE PITCHER AND
THE PLUTOCRAT

P. G. WODEHOUSE

The main difficulty in writing a story is to convey to the reader clearly yet tersely the natures and dispositions of one's leading characters. Brevity, brevity—that is the cry. Perhaps, after all, the playbill style is the best. In this drama of love, baseball, frenzied finance, and tainted millions, then, the principals are as follows, in their order of entry:

Isabel Rackstraw (a peach)

Clarence Van Puyster (a Greek god)

Old Man Van Puyster (a proud old aristocrat)

Old Man Rackstraw (a tainted millionaire)

More about Clarence later. For the moment let him go as a Greek god. There were other sides, too, to Old Man Rackstraw's character; but for the moment let him go as a Tainted Millionaire. Not that it is satisfactory. It is too mild. He was *the* Tainted Millionaire. The Tainted Millions of other Tainted Millionaires were as attar of roses compared with the Tainted Millions of Tainted Millionaire Rackstraw. He preferred his millions tainted. His attitude toward an untainted million was that of the sportsman toward the sitting bird. These things are purely a matter of taste. Some people like Limburger cheese.

It was at a charity bazaar that Isabel and Clarence first met. Isabel was presiding over the Billiken, Teddy Bear, and Fancy Goods stall. There she stood, that slim, radiant girl, buncoing the Younger Set out of its father's hard-earned with a smile that alone was nearly worth the money, when she observed, approaching, the handsomest man she had ever seen. It was—this is not one of those mystery stories—it was Clarence Van Puyster. Over the heads of the bevy of gilded youths who clustered round the stall their eyes met. A thrill ran through Isabel. She dropped her eyes. The next moment Clarence had bucked center; the Younger Set had shredded away like a mist; and he was leaning toward her, opening negotiations for the purchase of a yellow Teddy Bear at sixteen times its face value.

He returned at intervals during the afternoon. Over the second Teddy Bear they became friendly; over the third, intimate. He proposed as she was wrapping up the fourth Golliwog, and she gave him her heart and the parcel simultaneously. At six o'clock, carrying four Teddy Bears, seven photograph frames, five Golliwogs, and a Billiken, Clarence went home to tell the news to his father.

Clarence, when not at college, lived with his only surviving parent in an old red-brick house at the north end of Washington Square. The original Van Puyster had come over in Governor Stuyvesant's time in one of the then fashionable ninety-four-day boats. Those were the stirring days when they were giving away chunks of Manhattan Island in exchange for trading-stamps; for the bright brain which conceived the idea that the city might possibly at some remote date extend above Liberty Street had not come into existence. The original Van Puyster had acquired a square mile or so in the heart of things for ten dollars cash and a quarter interest in a pedler's outfit. "The Columbus Echo and Vespucci Intelligencer" gave him a column and a half under the heading: "Reckless Speculator. Prominent Citizen's Gamble in Land." On the proceeds of that deal his descendants had led quiet, peaceful lives ever since. If any of them ever did a day's work, the family records are silent on the point. Blood was their long suit, not Energy. They were plain, homely folk, with a refined distaste for wealth and vulgar hustle. They lived simply, without envy of their richer fellow citizens, on their three hundred thousand dollars a year. They asked no more. It enabled them to entertain on a modest scale; the boys could go to college, the girls buy an occasional new frock. They were satisfied.

Having dressed for dinner, Clarence proceeded to the library, where he found his father slowly pacing the room. Silver-haired old Vansuyther Van Puyster seemed wrapped in thought. And this was unusual, for he was not given to thinking. To be absolutely frank, the old man had just about enough brain to make a jay-bird fly crooked, and no more.

"Ah, my boy," he said, looking up as Clarence entered. "Let us go in to dinner. I have been awaiting you for some little time now. I was about to inquire as to your whereabouts. Let us be going."

Mr. Van Puyster always spoke like that. This was due to Blood.

Until the servants had left them to their coffee and cigarettes, the conversation was desultory and commonplace. But when the door had closed, Mr. Van Puyster leaned forward.

"My boy," he said quietly, "we are ruined."

Clarence looked at him inquiringly. "Ruined much?" he asked.

"Paupers," said his father. "I doubt if when all is over, I shall have much more than a bare fifty or sixty thousand dollars a year."

A lesser man would have betrayed agitation, but Clarence was a Van Puyster. He lit a cigarette.

"Ah," he said calmly. "How's that?"

Mr. Van Puyster toyed with his coffee-spoon.

"I was induced to speculate—rashly, I fear—on the advice of a man I chanced to meet at a public dinner, in the shares of a certain mine. I did not thoroughly understand the matter, but my acquaintance appeared to be well versed in such operations, so I allowed him to— and, well, in fact, to cut a long story short, I am ruined."

"Who was the fellow?"

"A man of the name of Rackstraw. Daniel Rackstraw."

"Daniel Rackstraw!"

Not even Clarence's training and traditions could prevent a slight start as he heard the name.

"Daniel Rackstraw," repeated his father. "A man, I fear, not entirely honest. In fact it seems that he has made a very large fortune by similar transactions. Friends of mine, acquainted with these matters, tell me his behavior toward me amounted practically to theft. However, for myself I care little. We can rough it, we of the old Van Puyster stock. If there is but fifty thousand a year left, well—I must make it serve.

It is for your sake that I am troubled, my poor boy. I shall be compelled to stop your allowance. I fear you will be obliged to adopt some profession." He hesitated for a moment. "In fact, work," he added.

Clarence drew at his cigarette.

"Work?" he echoed thoughtfully. "Well, of course, mind you, fellows *do* work. I met a man at the club only yesterday who knew a fellow who had met a man whose cousin worked."

He reflected for a while.

"I shall pitch," he said suddenly. "Pitch, my boy?"

"Sign on as a professional ballplayer."

His father's fine old eyebrows rose a little.

"But, my boy, er—the—ah—family name. Our—shall I say *noblesse oblige?* Can a Van Puyster pitch and not be defiled?"

"I shall take a new name," said Clarence. "I will call myself Brown." He lit another cigarette. "I can get signed on in a minute. McGraw will jump at me."

This was no idle boast. Clarence had had a good college education, and was now an exceedingly fine pitcher. It was a pleasing sight to see him, poised on one foot in the attitude of a Salome dancer, with one eye on the batter, the other gazing coldly at the man who was trying to steal third, uncurl abruptly like the main spring of a watch and sneak over a swift one. Under Clarence's guidance a ball could do practically everything except talk. It could fly like a shot from a gun, hesitate, take the first turning to the left, go up two blocks, take the second to the right, bound in mid-air like a jack-rabbit, and end by dropping as the gentle dew from heaven upon the plate beneath. Briefly, there was class to Clarence. He was the goods.

Scarcely had he uttered these momentous words when the butler entered with the announcement that he was wanted by a lady at the telephone.

It was Isabel.

Isabel was disturbed.

"Oh, Clarence," she cried, "my precious angel wonder-child, I don't know how to begin."

"Begin just like that," said Clarence approvingly. "It's fine. You can't beat it."

"Clarence, a terrible thing has happened. I told papa of our engagement, and he wouldn't hear of it. He was furious. He c-called you a b-b-b—

"A p-p-p—"

"That's a new one on me," said Clarence, wondering.

"A b-beggarly p-pauper. I knew you weren't well off, but I thought you had two or three millions. I told him so. But he said no, your father had lost all his money."

"It is too true, dearest," said Clarence. "I am a pauper. But I'm going to work. Something tells me I shall be rather good at work. I am going to work with all the accumulated energy of generations of ancestors who have never done a hand's turn. And some day when I—"

"Good-by," said Isabel hastily, "I hear papa coming."

The season during which Clarence Van Puyster pitched for the Giants is destined to live long in the memory of followers of baseball. Probably never in the history of the game has there been such persistent and widespread mortality among the more distant relatives of office-boys and junior clerks. Statisticians have estimated that if all the grandmothers alone who perished between the months of April and October that year could have been placed end to end they would have reached considerably further than Minneapolis. And it was Clarence who was responsible for this holocaust. Previous to the opening of the season skeptics had shaken their heads over the Giants' chances for the pennant. It had been assumed that as little new blood would be forthcoming as in other years, and that the fate of Our City would rest, as usual, on the shoulders of the whitehaired veterans who were boys with Lafayette.

And then, like a mentor, Clarence Van Puyster had flashed upon the world of fans, bugs, chewing-gum, and nuts (pea and human). In the opening game he had done horrid things to nine men from Boston; and from then onward, except for an occasional check, the Giants had never looked back.

Among the spectators who thronged the bleachers to watch Clarence perform there appeared week after week a little, gray, dried-up man, insignificant except for a certain happy choice of language in moments of emotion and an enthusiasm far surpassing that of the ordinary spectator. To the trained eye there is a subtle but well-marked difference between the fan, the bug, and—the last phase—the nut of the baseball world. This man was an undoubted nut. It was writ clear across his brow.

Fate had made Daniel Rackstraw—for it was he—a tainted million-aire, but at heart he was a baseball spectator. He never missed a game. His baseball museum had but one equal, that of Mr. Jacob Dodson of Detroit. Between them the two had cornered, at enormous expense, the curio market of the game. It was Rackstraw who had secured the glove worn by Neal Ball, the Cleveland shortstop, when he made the only unassisted triple play in the history of the game; but it was Dodson who possessed the bat which Hans Wagner used as a boy. The two men were friends, as far as rival connoisseurs can be friends; and Mr. Dodson, when at leisure, would frequently pay a visit to Mr. Rackstraw's country home, where he would spend hours gazing wistfully at the Neal Ball glove buoyed up only by the thought of the Wagner bat at home.

Isabel saw little of Clarence during the summer months, except from a distance. She contented herself with clipping photographs of him from the evening papers. Each was a little more unlike him than the last, and this lent variety to the collection. Her father marked her new-born enthusiasm for the national game with approval. It had been secretly a great grief to the old buccaneer that his only child did not know the difference between a bunt and a swat, and, more, did not seem to care to know. He felt himself drawn closer to her. An under-standing, as pleasant as it was new and strange, began to spring up between parent and child.

As for Clarence, how easy it would be to cut loose to practically an unlimited extent on the subject of his emotions at this time. One can figure him, after the game is over and the gay throng has dispersed, creeping moodily—but what's the use? Brevity. That is the cry, Brevity. Let us on.

The months sped by. August came and went, and September; and soon it was plain to even the casual follower of the game that, unless something untoward should happen, the Giants must secure the National League pennant. Those were delirious days for Daniel Rackstraw. Long before the beginning of October his voice had dwindled to a husky whisper. Deep lines appeared on his forehead; for it is an awful thing for a baseball nut to be compelled to root, in the very crisis of the season, purely by means of facial expression. In this time of affliction he found Isabel an ever-increasing comfort to him. Side by side they would sit at the Polo Grounds, and the old man's face would lose its drawn look, and light up, as her clear young soprano pealed out above the din, urging this player to slide for second, that to knock the stitching off the ball; or describing the umpire in no uncertain voice as a reincarnation of the late Mr. Jesse James.

Meanwhile, in the American League, Detroit had been heading the list with equal pertinacity; and in far-off Michigan Mr. Jacob Dodson's enthusiasm had been every whit as great as Mr. Rackstraw's in New York. It was universally admitted that when the championship series came to be played, there would certainly be something doing.

But, alas! How truly does Epictetus observe: "We know not what awaiteth us around the corner, and the hand that counteth its chickens ere they be hatched ofttimes graspeth but a lemon." The prophets who anticipated a struggle closer than any on record were destined to be proved false.

It was not that their judgment of form was at fault. By every law of averages the Giants and the Tigers should have been the two most evenly matched nines in the history of the game. In fielding there was nothing to choose between them. At hitting the Tigers held a slight superiority; but this was balanced by the inspired pitching of Clarence Van Puyster. Even the keenest supporters of either side were not confident. They argued at length, figuring out the odds with the aid of stubs of pencils and the backs of envelopes, but they were not confident. Out of all those frenzied millions two men alone had no doubts. Mr. Daniel Rackstraw said that he did not desire to be unfair to Detroit. He wished it to be clearly understood that in their own class the Tigers might quite possibly show to considerable advantage. In some rural league down South, for instance, he did not deny that they might sweep all before them. But when it came to competing with the Giants—Here words failed Mr. Rackstraw, and he had to rush to Wall Street and collect several tainted millions before he could recover his composure.

Mr. Jacob Dodson, interviewed by the Detroit "Weekly Rooter," stated that his decision, arrived at after a close and careful study of the work of both teams, was that the Giants had rather less chance in the forthcoming tourney than a lone gumdrop at an Eskimo tea party. It was his carefully considered opinion that in a contest with the Avenue B juniors the Giants might, with an effort, scrape home. But when it was a question of meeting a live team like Detroit—Here Mr. Dodson, shrugging his shoulders despairingly, sank back in his chair, and watchful secretaries brought him round with oxygen.

Throughout the whole country nothing but the approaching series was discussed. Wherever civilization reigned, and in Jersey City, one question alone was on every lip: Who would win? Octogenarians mumbled it. Infants lisped it. Tired business men, trampled under foot in the rush for the West Farms express, asked it of the ambulance attendants who carried them to hospital.

And then, one bright, clear morning, when all Nature seemed to smile, Clarence Van Puyster developed mumps.

New York was in a ferment. I could have wished to go into details to describe in crisp, burning sentences the panic that swept like a tornado through a million homes. A little encouragement, the slightest softening of the editorial austerity, and the thing would have been done. But no. Brevity. That was the cry. Brevity. Let us on.

The Tigers met the Giants at the Polo Grounds, and for five days the sweat of agony trickled unceasingly down the corrugated foreheads of the patriots who sat on the bleachers. The men from Detroit, freed from the fear of Clarence, smiled grim smiles and proceeded to knock holes through the fence. It was in vain that the home fielders skimmed like swallows around the diamond. They could not keep the score down. From start to finish the Giants were a beaten side.

Broadway during that black week was a desert. Gloom gripped Lobster Square. In distant Harlem red-eyed wives faced silently scowling husbands at the evening meal, and the children were sent early to bed. Newsboys called the extras in a whisper.

Few took the tragedy more nearly to heart than Daniel Rackstraw. Each afternoon found him more deeply plunged in sorrow. On the last day, leaving the ground with the air of a father mourning over some prodigal son, he encountered Mr. Jacob Dodson of Detroit.

Now, Mr. Dodson was perhaps the slightest bit shy on the finer feelings. He should have respected the grief of a fallen foe. He should have abstained from exulting. But he was in too exhilarated a condition to be magnanimous. Sighting Mr. Rackstraw, he addressed himself joyously to the task of rubbing the thing in. Mr. Rackstraw listened in silent anguish.

"If we had had Brown—" he said at length. "That's what they all say," whooped Mr. Dodson.

"Brown! Who's Brown?"

"If we had had Brown, we should have—" He paused. An idea had flashed upon his overwrought mind. "Dodson," he said, "listen here. Wait till Brown is well again, and let us play this thing off again for anything you like a side in my private park."

Mr. Dodson reflected.

"You're on," he said. "What side bet? A million? Two million? Three?"

Mr. Rackstraw shook his head scornfully.

"A million? Who wants a million? I'll put on my Neal Ball glove against your Hans Wagner bat. The best of three games. Does that go?"

"I should say it did," said Mr. Dodson joyfully. "I've been wanting that glove for years. It's like finding it in one's Christmas stocking."

"Very well," said Mr. Rackstraw. "Then let's get it fixed up."

Honestly, it is but a dog's life, that of the shortstory writer. I particularly wished at this point to introduce a description of Mr. Rackstraw's country home and estate, featuring the private ballpark with its fringe of noble trees. It would have served a double purpose, not only charming the lover of nature, but acting as a fine stimulus to the youth of the country, showing them the sort of home they would be able to buy some day if they worked hard and saved their money. But no. You shall have three guesses as to what was the cry. You give it up? It was "Brevity! Brevity!" Let us on.

The two teams arrived at the Rackstraw house in time for lunch. Clarence, his features once more reduced to thier customary finely chiseled proportions, alighted from the automobile with a swelling heart. He could see nothing of Isabel, but that did not disturb him. Letters had passed between the two. Clarence had warned her not to embrace him in public, as McGraw would not like it; and Isabel accordingly had arranged a tryst among the noble trees which fringed the ballpark.

I will pass lightly over the meeting of the two lovers. I will not describe the dewy softness of their eyes, the catching of their breath, their murmured endearments. I could, mind you. It is at just such descriptions that I am particularly happy. But I have grown discouraged. My spirit is broken. It is enough to say that Clarence had reached a level of emotional eloquence rarely met with among pitchers of the National League, when Isabel broke from him with a startled exclamation, and vanished behind a tree; and, looking over his shoulder, Clarence observed Mr. Daniel Rackstraw moving toward him.

It was evident from the millionaire's demeanor that he had seen nothing. The look on his face was anxious, but not wrathful. He sighted Clarence, and hurried up to him.

"Say, Brown," he said. "I've been looking for you. I want a word with you."

"A thousand, if you wish it," said Clarence courteously.

"Now, see here," said Mr. Rackstraw. "I want to explain to you just what this ball game means to me. Don't run away with the idea I've had you fellows down to play an exhibition game just to keep me merry and bright. If the Giants win today, it means that I shall be able to hold up my head again and look my fellow man in the face, instead of crawling around on my stomach and feeling like thirty cents. Do you get that?"

"I am hep," replied Clarence with simple dignity. "And not only that," went on the millionaire.

"There's more to it. I have put up my Neal Ball glove against Mr. Dodson's Wagner bat as a side bet. You understand what that means? It means that either you win or my life is soured for keeps. See?"

"I have got you," said Clarence.

"Good. Then what I wanted to say was this. Today is your day for pitching as you've never pitched before. Everything depends on whether you make good or not. With you pitching like mother used to make it, the Giants are some nine. Otherwise they are Nature's citrons. It's one thing or the other. It's all up to you. Win, and there's twenty thousand dollars waiting for you above what you share with the others."

Clarence waved his hand deprecatingly.

"Mr. Rackstraw," he said, "keep your dough. I care nothing for money."

"You don't?" cried the millionaire. "Then you ought to exhibit yourself in a dime museum."

"All I ask of you," proceeded Clarence, "is your consent to my engagement to your daughter."

Mr. Rackstraw looked sharply at him.

"Repeat that," he said. "I don't think I quite got it."

"All I ask is your consent to my engagement to your daughter."

"Young man," said Mr. Rackstraw, not without a touch of admiration, "you have gall."

"My friends have sometimes said so," said Clarence.

"And I admire gall. But there is a limit. That limit you have passed so far that you'd need to look for it with a telescope."

"You refuse your consent."

"I never said you weren't a clever guesser."

"Why?"

Mr. Rackstraw laughed. One of those nasty, sharp, metallic laughs that hit you like a bullet.

"How would you support my daughter?"

"I was thinking that you would help to some extent."

"You were, were you?"

"I was."

"Oh?"

Mr. Rackstraw emitted another of those laughs. "Well," he said, "it's off. You can take that as coming from an authoritative source. No wedding-bells for you."

Clarence drew himself up, fire flashing from his eyes and a bitter smile curving his expressive lips.

"And no Wagner bat for you!" he cried.

Mr. Rackstraw started as if some strong hand had plunged an auger into him.

"What!" he shouted.

Clarence shrugged his superbly modeled shoulders in silence.

"Say," said Mr. Rackstraw, "you wouldn't let a little private difference like that influence you any in a really important thing like this ball game, would you?"

"I would."

"You would hold up the father of the girl you love?"

"Every time."

"Her white-haired old father?"

"The color of his hair would not affect me."

"Nothing would move you?"

"Nothing."

"Then, by George, you're just the son-in-law I want. You shall marry Isabel; and I'll take you into partnership this very day. I've been looking for a good, husky bandit like you for years. You make Dick Turpin look like a preliminary three-round bout. My boy, we'll be the greatest team, you and I, that ever hit Wall Street."

"Papa!" cried Isabel, bounding happily from behind her tree.

Mr. Rackstraw joined their hands, deeply moved, and spoke in low, vibrant tones:

"Play ball!"

Little remains to be said, but I am going to say it, if it snows. I am at my best in these tender scenes of idyllic domesticity.

Four years have passed. Once more we are in the Rackstraw home. A lady is corning down the stairs, leading by the hand her little son. It is Isabel. The years have dealt lightly with her. She is still the same stately, beautiful creature whom I would have described in detail long ago if I had been given half a chance. At the foot of the stairs the child stops and points at a small, wooden object in a glass case.

"Wah?" he said.

"That?" says Isabel. "That is the bat Mr. Wagner used to use when he was a little boy."

She looks at a door on the left of the hall, and puts a finger to her lip.

"Hush!" she says. "We must be quiet. Daddy and grandpa are busy in there cornering wheat."

And softly mother and child go out into the sunlit garden.

THE SLIDE OF
PAUL REVERE

GRANTLAND RICE

LISTEN, fanatics, and you shall hear
Of the midnight slide of Paul Revere;
How he scored from first on an outfield drive
By a dashing spring and a headlong dive
'Twas the greatest play pulled off that year.

Now the home of poets and potted beans,
Of Emersonian ways and means
In baseball epic has oft been sung
Since the days of Criger and old Cy Young;
But not even fleet, deer-footed Bay
Could have pulled off any such fancy play
As the slide of P. Revere, which won
The famous battle of Lexington.

The Yanks and the British were booked that trip
In a scrap for the New World championship;
But the British landed a bit too late,
So the game didn't open till half past eight,

And Paul Revere was dreaming away
When the umpire issued his call for play.

On, on they fought, 'neath the Boston moon,
As the British figured, "Not yet, but soon;"
For the odds were against the Yanks that night,
With Paul Revere blocked away from the fight
And the grandstand gathering groaned in woe,
While a sad wail bubbled from Rooters' Row.

But wait! Hist! Hearken! and likewise hark!
What means that galloping near the park?
What means that cry of a man dead sore?
"Am I too late? Say, what's the score?"
And echo answered both far and near,
As the rooters shouted: "There's Paul Revere!"

Oh how sweetly that moon did shine
When P. Revere took the coaching line!
He woke up the grandstand from its trance
And made the bleachers get up and dance;
He joshed the British with robust shout
Until they booted the ball about.
He whooped and he clamored all over the lot,
Till the score was tied in a Gordian knot.

Now, in this part of the "Dope Recooked"
Are the facts which history overlooked—
How Paul Revere came to bat that night
And suddenly ended the long-drawn fight;
How he singled to center, and then straightway
Dashed on to second like Harry Bay;

Kept traveling on, with the speed of a bird,
Till he whizzed like a meteor, rounding third.
"Hold back, you lobster!" but all in vain
The coachers shouted in tones of pain;
For Paul kept on with a swinging stride,
And he hit the ground when they hollered: "Slide!"

Spectacular players may come and go
In the hurry of Time's swift ebb and flow;
But never again will there be one
Like the first American "hit and run."
And as long as the old game lasts you'll hear
Of the midnight slide of P. Revere.

SOURCES

"Why Base Ball Has Become Our National Game" by Albert G. Spalding. From *America's National Game* (1911).

"The Model Base Ball Player" by Henry Chadwick. From *Ball Players Chronicle* (1867).

"Casey at the Bat" by Ernest Lawrence Thayer. From *The San Francisco Examiner* (1888).

"Casey's Revenge" by Grantland Rice. From *Base-Ball Ballads* (1910).

"The Color Line" by Sol White. From *Sol White's Official Guide: History of Colored Baseball* (1907).

"A Whale of a Pastime" by Brig. Gen. Frederick Funston. From *Harper's Round Table* (1894).

"The Rube's Honeymoon" by Zane Grey. From *The Red-Headed Outfield* (1920).

"How I Pitched the First Curve" by William Arthur (Candy) Cummings (1908).

"Discovering Cy Young" by Alfred H. Spink. From *The National Game* (1911).

"Varsity Frank" by Burt L. Standish. From *Frank Merriwell at Yale* (1903).

"Baseball Joe's Winning Throw" by Lester Chadwick. From *Baseball Joe of the Silver Stars* (1912).

"Mr. Dooley on Baseball" by Finley Peter Dunne. From *Mr. Dooley on Making a Will and Other Necessary Evils* (1919).

"Jinxes and What They Mean to a Ball-Player" by Christy Mathewson. From *Pitching in a Pinch* (1912).

"One Down, 713 to Go" by Damon Runyon. From *The New York American* (1915).

"How I Lost the 1915 World Series" by Grover Cleveland Alexander. From *Baseball* (1915).

"The Crab" by Gerald Beaumont. From *Hearts and the Diamond* (1921).

"My Roomy" by Ring Lardner. From *The Saturday Evening Post* (1914).

"The Longest Game" by Ralph D. Blanpied. From *The New York Times* (1920).

"Fullerton Says Seven Members of the White Sox Will Be Missing Next Spring" by Hugh Fullerton. From *The Chicago Herald and Examiner* (1919).

"His Own Stuff" by Charles E. Van Loan. From *Score by Innings* (1919).

"The Pitcher and the Plutocrat" by P. G. Wodehouse. From *Colliers* (1910).

"The Slide of Paul Revere" by Grantland Rice. From *BaseBall Ballads* (1910).